Praise for *Soar!* and Zoro

Zoro rocks—figuratively and literally! His book *Soar!* is filled with practical, godly wisdom that will enable you to discover your gifts, develop them, and deploy them to make a difference in the world the way God intended. If you're wondering why you're here, and what your purpose is, read this book. It's sure to lead you on an exciting adventure to a life of intention, integrity, and impact.

Kevin Sorbo
Actor, director, producer, and author

Zoro's latest book is what millions in today's ever-changing world are asking for: a well-defined plan you can do right now to move forward with your life. It's like a college education with an added rare and secret ingredient—your next steps to take. Written by a world-renowned drummer and author who's proven it himself, *Soar!* will help you do just that!

Michael W. Smith
Grammy Award-winning recording artist

Zoro's contagious enthusiasm pulsates through these pages and provides hope that regardless of your past or your current circumstances, you can discover the sounds of a different Drummer. You'll find no pious platitudes here, no "pie in the sky." *Soar!* contains workable solutions to your everyday, down-to-earth problems. This book not only sings, it *flies!*

braham
author

Zoro's new book, *Soar!*, is a p⬚ depth. It's rare that a book is this inte ⬚ ...structional, and inspiring at the same time. This ⬚ will recommend to everyone I know, regardless of their spiritual maturity.

Rick Joyner
Bestselling author, conference speaker, educator

Zoro has a tremendous passion for ministry and sharing the gospel. When we had him as a guest on our program, I immediately connected with his desire to communicate God's truths in a real down-to-earth way. His story is one of persistence, diligence, and faith.

Joyce Meyer
Bestselling author and Bible teacher

I hate poverty. It destroys hope and kills dreams. My friend Zoro knows this firsthand; so do I. But I love that as a boy Zoro didn't allow poverty or hardship to defeat him. He conquered them. And now he has soared to amazing heights. In this wonderful book, he tells us how. Zoro has earned the right to do that. Letting go of the old and damaging, and reaching out to the new and challenging, he shows us the way. If you know deep in your soul you were made for more, you owe it to yourself to devour this message. God's best for you is waiting—it's your move!

Dr. Wess Stafford
President Emeritus
Compassion International

Zoro's latest book is a practical and profound "how-to" presentation that helps us focus on what matters most as we search for significance in a complex and confusing world. Being raised by a single mom who faced poverty and overwhelming obstacles, and then achieving the pinnacle of success, makes his inspiring story and gospel message all the more poignant. A fast-paced, dynamic read and a great guide for anyone looking to Soar in life!

Kevin Palau
President
Luis Palau Association

Zoro's heart, discipline, and passion are what propelled him to greatness... His music and life lessons are about using your God-given talents to the maximum.

Lenny Kravitz
Grammy Award-winning recording artist and actor

Zoro has written a textbook for life that everyone should read. My prayer for Zoro and this book is that everyone who sees it or hears about it will not miss the chance to read it.

Ken Barun
Senior Vice President
Billy Graham Evangelistic Association

From my first encounter with Zoro, his zeal has been motivating, powerful, and infectious. I hope Zoro's unique experiences and the wisdom he has acquired through the years will be a blessing to you, as I believe Zoro to be one of the true gifts to pure artistry.

Stephen Baldwin
Actor, filmmaker, and author

Zoro reminds us of the potential for greatness that lies inside each of us and shows you step-by-step what it actually takes to achieve excellence in all areas of your life.

Kathie Lee Gifford
Cohost of NBC's Today Show and former host of
Live! with Regis and Kathie Lee

Zoro is one of the best in the business. His wisdom goes beyond music, however. He offers life lessons that will encourage anyone.

Toby Mac
Christian recording artist

This book is an excellent and practical guide on how to be everything that you were meant to be. It's a "must read."

Joe Watkins
MSNBC political analyst

You don't meet guys like Zoro often. He's an extremely talented artist with a heart for helping people reach their potential.

Jason Kennedy
Weekend anchor, E! News and actor

Zoro is a master. He has walked boldly, faithfully, and with the confidence of victory being his reward. Lock into Zoro's insight and wisdom, which only the God of heaven could impart.

Peter Furler
Songwriter, artist, producer, and former lead singer of Newsboys

People were really blessed by Zoro's ministry.

Harry Thomas
Creation Festival

I want to encourage you pastors, youth and young adult pastors, and worship leaders to get Zoro to come and be a blessing to your ministry.

Marcus Lamb
Founder, Daystar Television

As Zoro made his way onto our set it was evident we were in the presence of a man after God's own heart.

Dr. Morris Cerullo
Helpline!

When you look at Zoro you see a new side of God. When you listen to his story, you hear the heart of the Father.

The 700 Club

Zoro is one of the most unique people I have ever met, and I mean that in the most positive sense possible. He is an amazing combination of artist, educator, devoted family man, friend, and encourager. His book is sure to challenge and inspire you in life-changing ways. I encourage anyone looking to live his or her life with a greater sense of purpose to read it. I am grateful to call Zoro a friend. He is truly one of a kind.

Lincoln Brewster
Recording artist and songwriter

In today's culture, one rarely looks to celebrities as role models or for inspiration. Zoro works to inspire a generation of young people with reliable standards of right and wrong based on faith and with good advice on how to turn dreams into reality.

Gary Bauer
President
American Values

Zoro may seem like another rock star drummer. But once you talk with him, it becomes quickly apparent that Zoro is an anointed man of God. Zoro is a phenomenal husband, father, musician, speaker, and author, with wisdom about how to do all these things with excellence. His words and thoughts hold great value.

Ed Cash
Producer and songwriter for such artists as Amy Grant, Chris Tomlin, and Steven Curtis Chapman

Zoro is one spectacular individual. His principles are solid, his thinking is clear, and his passion for life and others is obvious. How can you not like a book from a guy who is rooting so much for you to win in life?

Bruce Adolph
Publisher
Christian Musician Magazine

From the very first time I met Z, it was apparent we both share a passion for Christ and a mission to empower kids. His testimony as a former little brother in the Big Brothers Big Sisters program is both powerful and entertaining. This book displays the depth of the man and his dedication to taking his own unique gifting to the maximum and inspiring others to their own level of greatness.

Lowell Perry, Jr.
Chief Executive Officer
Big Brothers Big Sisters of Middle Tennessee

SOAR!

YOU WERE MEANT TO LIVE FOR SO MUCH MORE

9 Proven Keys for Unlocking
Your Limitless Potential

SOAR!
9 Proven Keys for Unlocking Your Limitless Potential

Published by:
Emerge Publishing, LLC
9521B Riverside Parkway, Suite 243
Tulsa, Oklahoma 74137
888.407.4447
www.EmergePublishing.com

emerge
p u b l i s h i n g
TULSA, OKLAHOMA

Cover and interior design: Heather Huether | www.theeastcogroup.com
Author back cover photo: Matthew Fried

Library of Congress Cataloging-in-Publication Data

BISAC Category: SEL027000 SELF-HELP / Personal Growth / Success
              REL012120 RELIGION / Christian Life / Spiritual Growth

ISBN: 978-1-943127-23-8 Softcover
ISBN: 978-1-943127-24-5 Digital

Printed in Canada

First Edition First Printing

This book is dedicated to the three incomparable women in my life who have enabled me to soar! In order of their appearance, they are my loving, and dearly departed mother, Maria; my incredibly kindhearted sister, Patricia; and my beautiful and precious wife, Renee. I simply could not have taken flight without your extravagant love that has enriched my life with unspeakable joy. Collectively, you are the wind beneath my wings, and all that I am is all that you are.

It is your genuine faithfulness that has kept my hope intact, dreams alive, and heart soft. Truly, there has been no sweeter outpouring of God's love toward me, than the women He chose to love, nurture, and inspire me. You are the fragrance of His goodness, and I live to make you all proud.

To my children, Jarod and Jordan, you are my treasure upon this earth and the true riches of God's eternal glory. The Lord smiled upon me the day He chose me to be your father. It is my heart's desire to see each of you soar and impact this world in a most profound way. You both have a great destiny that God has prepared for you, but you must seize it with faith, fortitude, and fervor. May this book serve as the baton I now pass on to you, which contains the blueprints for your inevitable success!

With a never-ending love and an eternal sense of gratitude, Daddy

Acknowledgments

*There is no such thing as a self-made man. We are made up
of thousands of others. Everyone who has ever done a kind
deed for us, or spoken one word of encouragement to us,
has entered into the make-up of our character
and our thoughts, as well as our success.*
~ George Matthew Adams, American newspaper columnist

Father, Son, and Holy Spirit

First and foremost, I give praise to God the Father for the gift of life and all the creative abilities He has bestowed upon mankind. To the Holy Spirit for teaching me how to fulfill the dreams the Father has placed in my heart, and for giving me the strength and courage necessary to pursue those visions to completion. To my Lord and Savior Jesus Christ, I thank You for Your never-ending love and enduring the cross so I could have eternal life and experience victory and abundance in this one.

Wife, Children, and Mother

I thank my precious and incredible wife, Renee, for her love, support, faithfulness, and for all she does to bless my life and the lives of our children. Her spirit of excellence is unmatched and makes it possible for me to do everything I do. Thanks for believing in me beautiful and for standing by my side all these years through every kind of storm and season. Thank you, Jarod and Jordan, for filling my life with unspeakable joy and inspiration; it is a privilege to be your father. I thank God for allowing me to be a steward over your lives each and every day.

I thank my dearly departed mother, Maria, for being the absolute light of my life and greatest mother a boy could have. She was a tremendous source of love, encouragement, and inspiration and it was truly an honor to be her son. None of my success would have been possible without her.

Thank you my dear, sweet mother for filling my heart with big dreams and high hopes, for believing in me the way you did, and for being the wind beneath my wings. God showed me His great love when He chose you to be my mother!

Family

I extend my deepest gratitude to all my brothers and sisters. The six of you have played an integral role in what I have been able to achieve, and you have enriched my life through the many vast experiences and incredible adventures we have shared together. Thank you, Armando, for being my protector; Maria, for teaching me how to stand up and fight; Ricardo, for the greatest of adventures; Patricia, for investing in me like no other and showing me the world; Bobby, for being my absolute best friend; and Lisa, for being my pal and always laughing at my jokes.

I would also like to give special thanks to my niece Lydia Bravo for all her love, support, advice, and tremendous friendship through the years! Love and thanks go to all the rest of my nieces and nephews—Anna, Corina, Linda, Armando Jr., Anthony, Travis, Gina, Jordyn, Calvyn, Stephanie, André, and Angelina, for being who you are.

Thanks to my in-laws Wil and Sandy Strong for their unbelievable faith and for being such a tremendous blessing through the years in every way. Also special thanks to my brother-in-law, George Weiss, for his generosity and kindness through the years.

Editorial and Design

My deepest gratitude goes to my editor, writing coach, and friend Lisa Cieslewicz for helping me put this manuscript together from start to finish. Her invaluable insight, excruciating attention to detail, godly council, and unwavering faith in me and what God has called me to do has made this book what it is. It simply would not have been possible without her love, support, generosity, and incredible expertise. Thanks, Lisa, for being among the very first to support my ministry vision. You're a diamond in a world full of rocks!

Another heartfelt thanks to Marcus Brotherton for his beautiful final touches on the manuscript and for sharing his amazing insight, guidance, and enthusiasm. Special thanks goes to my friend Holt Vaughn for his generosity, invaluable insight, direction, and for believing and investing in me. Thanks to Heather Huether at the Eastco Group for her incredible cover design and stellar layout of this book. I would also like to extend my sincere appreciation to Georgia Varozza for her impeccable job with the final copy editing of this manuscript. You put the final shimmer of excellence on my work, for which I am thrilled. Thanks so much for allowing me to be a recipient of your talent and wonderful spirit! You brought the book to the final inning of the game. Special thanks to Christian Ophus at Emerge Publishing for his immense help in getting this book to Soar!

Believers and Investors

There are no words that can properly express my gratitude to the following very special people for believing in me and investing in me in their own personal and genuine way. Their love, support, prayers, and encouragement have allowed me to carry out the work that God has called me to do. I hope all that I've tried to do to impact the world in a positive way will suffice as payment toward your generous investment in me. It has been my greatest desire to make you all proud of me and to spend my life on something that will outlast it.

Thank you very much to Patricia Bravo Weiss, Lenny Kravitz, Jerry Hammack, Bill and Robin Siren, Marty and Tracy Layton, Kim and Jane Clement and the entire Kim Clement ministry team, Bob and Jennifer Cashier, Jim and Marlece Watson, Holt Vaughn and the entire team at The Eastco Group, Miles Fonda and Erik Ticen at The Eastco Group, Scott and Julie Spiewak, Greg Johnson, Beverly, Lolita and Osama Afifi, Rick Joyner, Russ and Christine Miller, Robert Jolly, Kevin Sorbo, Ken Barun and the Billy Graham Evangelistic Association, The Luis Palau Evangelistic Association, Wes Stafford and Compassion International, Big Brothers Big Sisters of America, Belmont University in Nashville, TN, Michael W. Smith, Chaz Corzine, Bill Johnson, Amy Hammond Hagberg, Keith and Heidi Hershey, Cheryl Benedick, Carlo Krouzian, Anthony and Rosanne Albanese, Steve Trudell, Allen Rhodes, Eric Rhodes, Vic Comstock, Brian Jacobs, Lisa McDonald, Scott Jette, Shirley Alecock, Lu Hanessian, Alexis McKinney, Michael and Kristi Hamrick, Bruce Adolph, Matt Kees, Phil Potor, Josh D'Aubin, Danielle Fairweather, Sammi Potts, Sam Eisenberg, Alex Dowidchuk, Terryl and Heidi Zerby, Joyce, Dave and Danny Meyer, Marcus and Joni Lamb, David and Rhonda Kemp, Tim Fogerty, Kyle Prins, Dennis and Anita Tinerino, Angus and Catherine Keith, Jusden Aumand, Lauren Green, Jerry and Barb Andreas, Steve and Sally Petree, Debbie Burleigh, Ken and Becky Wagner, Rick Cua, Lindell Cooley and Grace Church Nashville, Scott MacLeod and Thunder School Nashville, Gary and Faye Asher, Steve Russo, Victoria Kemper, Jamie Warren and Forrest Walden at Iron Tribe Fitness, Jason Kennedy, Greg Lennox, Jules Follet, Bob and Joyce Robertson, Ken and Lisa Abraham, Jon and Shari Godly, Janet White, Tim and Karlene Smith and Cornerstone Christian Center, Michele Shepherd, Jackie Monaghan, Doug, David and the entire Coe family, and David Curtis.

I also extend my deepest gratitude to my friend Frank DaMatto, a man who picked me up when I was down, a man who taught me the meaning of the word faith and how to believe and trust God, a man who made my life better because of his. I'll see you in heaven, Frank!

Mentors and Molders

Much love, honor, and respect go out to my early mentors who played key roles in shaping me during my formative years. I thank each of you from the bottom of my heart for the love you so faithfully demonstrated to me. Each of you carries a very special place in my heart. You are the biggest part of me and helped me become the person I am today: Pearl Jones; Reverend Williamson from Faith Baptist Church in

Grants Pass, Oregon; Jack and Chris Smith and the staff at Wilderness Trails Camp in Oregon; James Worthington; Joe Kantola; Eric Christianson; Bill and Beverly Large; the Big Brothers Big Sisters of America program; Kent Clinkinbeard; Donn Essig; and Ralph Johnson and Al McKay of Earth, Wind & Fire. I would also like to thank the following churches for helping me in my greatest time of need: Our Lady of Victory, St. Anne's, Christian Assembly, and Overcomers Faith Church.

Equipment Manufacturers and Endorsements

I wish to thank the following musical instrument manufacturers for their contribution to my life's work as a musician, author, educator, and speaker. Your invaluable support of all I've endeavored to do has allowed me the privilege of impacting so many people around the world. It is an honor and pleasure to represent you in all I do and to play your magnificent equipment. Thanks for your friendship and making the finest equipment in the world. DW drums, Sabian cymbals, Latin Percussion, Evans drumheads, Vic Firth sticks, Audix microphones, and SKB cases.

Friends and Allies

The truth is that there are countless people who have made this book possible in one way or another, as it is the culmination of all that I have experienced, learned, and accomplished thus far. Therefore, I am grateful to each individual who has contributed to my life's journey.

From the bottom of my heart I thank all of those who have loved, sown, taught, helped, encouraged, and forgiven me in any way shape or form. This includes every individual and organization that has ever invited to me to speak, teach, preach, perform, and share my gifts with those entrusted unto you. Each of you in your own special way constitutes the thread that embroiders the overall fabric of my life.

Contents

Introduction

If we all did the things we are capable of doing,
we would literally astound ourselves.
~ Thomas Edison, American inventor and businessman

I'm living my dream.

Are you living yours?

I've spent my entire adult life so far being a professional rock and roll drummer. I've set the groove for some of the greatest recording artists of our time. Hanging with music legends, movie stars, super models, political dignitaries, famous athletes, mega-church pastors, and billionaires of business is all part of my job.

But though I regularly spend time among some of the most successful people in the world, I came from the humblest of beginnings. At one point in my childhood, my five siblings, our mother, and I lived in a dilapidated 13-foot-long trailer (and a 1962 Chevy Nova because there wasn't enough room for all of us to sleep in the trailer). I've also ministered among the poorest of the poor in various third-world countries, and I've seen how having a lot of money doesn't necessarily make you a success.

These vastly different experiences have enabled me to relate to people from all walks of life, and I've learned many things about true success along the way.

Perhaps you're a high school student wondering what direction your life is going to take after graduation.

Or maybe you're a college graduate ready to take on the world but have no idea how you're going to achieve success.

Maybe you're an adult who doesn't feel like you're doing what you were born to do.

Perhaps you are a seasoned professional who feels trapped and disenchanted with life.

Or maybe you're a parent whose youngest child has just flown the coop and now you anxiously wonder about this next season of life.

Whatever your story, there is one thing that unifies us all: the desire to reach our potential and live a life of fulfillment.

We are all meant to soar!

Throughout my global adventures, I've been given a bird's-eye view of some of the most fascinating, perplexing, and successful people on the planet. I've witnessed at close range the astonishingly good, the incredibly bad, and the brutally ugly. And it has led me on a quest to uncover the secrets of a life filled with meaning, purpose, success, and satisfaction. What I have learned can transform your thinking and potentially change the course of your life.

During my encounters with the famous, affluent, and powerful, I've found many to be unfulfilled and dissatisfied with life despite their tremendous accomplishments. I've also spent time with people who aren't celebrities, rich, or influential but who wished to unlock their potential and achieve something significant during their lifetime.

In both scenarios, I discovered there were vital essentials missing from their lives that kept them grounded and unable to get what they desperately longed for.

These revelations were the inspiration for the nine life principles of *Soar!*. Each principle is meant to build upon the next so you can use this book as a launching pad for your life to take flight in amazing ways.

The principles have enabled me to unlock my own potential, live out many of the dreams God placed in my heart, and experience personal fulfillment that is not dependent upon external circumstances.

I am confident these life lessons will do the same for you. As you read, embrace, and apply each of these tenets to your personal situation, you can experience powerful transformation that will help you become everything God created you to be.

Through my lifetime, I have walked out the nine life principles shared in this book. And I will continue to do so, as there is much more I hope to accomplish.

They are time-tested universal truths that apply to all of us, regardless of your particular faith or religious affiliation. But remember, no matter what your belief system, you will never stumble upon your divine destiny by accident. To uncover this priceless treasure, you must hunger after it with all of our heart, mind, and soul.

For most of my life, I have maintained a burning desire to unearth my own divine mission and impact this world in a positive manner with the gifts and talents I have been given. It is my earnest desire to help others do the same.

At this point, you might be like many others—wondering what the difference is between gifts and talents. For our purposes in this book, let's simplify the definitions.

God pre-wired gifts and talents into you when He created you. A gift can be thought of as an ability to excel in a particular area with minimal effort. This natural gift will flow out of you with the greatest of ease. Think of someone who sings beautifully but has never had vocal lessons.

Talent can be seen as a natural seed of potential to excel within a particular arena. Even though you may possess this talent, you will need to develop it. Talents require training to maximize their potential. Olympic and professional athletes are great examples.

The reason God chose to give you gifts and talents in the first place was so you could make a quantifiable difference in the world and enhance the lives of others. Your gifts and talents add a much-needed dimension to our world through the vibrancy and color you bring to every situation where you allow yourself to be used.

As you read *Soar!*, I pray that the practical wisdom and compelling stories contained within these pages will inspire you and help you take flight as God intends.

FLY LIKE AN EAGLE

Soarin' Over California is my all-time favorite theme park ride. This ingenious Disney California Adventure attraction puts you in a simulated hang glider so you can "soar" above the many gorgeous landscapes and notable landmarks of the Golden State.

It's an epic and exhilarating adventure that fills me with a sense of awe and wonder. Most importantly, it reaffirms my belief that God intends for us to experience life with this same sense of adventure.

From the beginning of time, mankind has been fascinated with the idea of taking flight. Whether flying kites or throwing paper airplanes, our obsession with flight begins in early childhood. Many of us even dream of flying.

And who hasn't watched eagles soar gracefully through the air and thought how awesome it would be to defy gravity in such a manner. There's definitely something inherent in the hearts of women and men, boys and girls that beckons us to take flight. Although we're on terra firma most of the time, our spirits long to reach toward the heavens.

Regardless of age, background, or season of life, each of us entertains this secret desire to ascend to higher heights. This is because God will simply not allow us to be satisfied with the mundane and uneventful life for which so many of us settle. We were meant to soar!

Refuse to be average. Let your heart soar as high as it will.
~ A. W. Tozer, American preacher and author

Eagles are fascinating and inspiring. The majestic creatures seemingly fly without effort or care. But the truth is, eagles cannot fly without the assistance of elements beyond their control. To experience liftoff, eagles must face into a headwind and rely on air currents to flow over and under them.

Just as there are natural laws God put in place that allow eagles to take flight, there are also supernatural laws He set in motion which allow us to soar spiritually, personally, and vocationally.

In the same way eagles need air currents and wind to maintain altitude, we need God's assistance to move confidently into the future He has prepared for us. All birds must leave their nests to fly and so must we.

When we choose to walk with God by faith, He lifts us into a marvelous adventure tailored specifically for each of us. Unlike Soarin' Over California, the journey He has prepared for us is not simulated. It's the real deal and demands we do more than just soak in the view from a comfortable seat.

God's action-packed, real-life journey takes us through majestic valleys and mountains. And it leads us into dry deserts, dense forests, thick brush, and through every kind of wilderness terrain.

God allows us to view the landscape of life from every vantage point so we can know Him intimately through the process and fully appreciate the vastness of our journey. Our life is the greatest excursion of all time and God gives us the privilege of soaring with Him.

If we never had the courage to take a leap of faith,
we'd be cheating God out of a chance to mount us up
on wings like eagles and watch us soar.
~ Jen Stephens, American author

SOARING WITHOUT LIMITS

How to Begin Reaching Your Potential

One can never consent to creep when one feels the impulse to soar.

~ Helen Keller, American author and political activist

My childhood was an extremely challenging one, filled with great adversity, emotional anguish, and poverty. The future held little promise of achievement. I felt cheated and ill-equipped for success of any kind.

For starters, my father abandoned me when I was six months old. My mother had the incredibly difficult task of raising seven children without the support of a husband or extended family. Life in the low-income neighborhoods of Los Angeles where I grew up was one great struggle heaped upon another.

We were often evicted from our apartments for having too many occupants; by the time I reached fourth grade, we had moved 23 times. Since we could rarely afford to rent a U-Haul truck, I helped my family move what few possessions we owned in my Radio Flyer wagon.

Stability was not a word in our vocabulary. I grew up feeling rejected, inadequate, disqualified, overlooked, and ashamed. I didn't feel as smart, talented, or handsome as other boys, and certainly not as privileged.

Yet despite being bombarded with feelings of worthlessness and incompetence, in my heart of hearts I felt there was something beyond my current plight that was greater than my circumstances.

In essence, I felt the presence of God drawing me to a place of faith and hope. Against all odds, I chose to believe that somewhere in the future a great destiny awaited me.

Little did my tender, childish brain know—while beating on Folgers coffee cans to make music—that a natural gifting of rhythm would someday lead me on an extraordinary adventure that would become my adult life.

Who could have imagined that the scrawny little shaver who scuffled through the concrete jungle of Los Angeles and scrounged up used clothes from the Goodwill drop box would become a man who would perform before royalty?

It was unfathomable to think an invisible, forgotten, inner-city poor child would one day be a guest on the most expensive privately owned yacht in the world. But it has happened.

The teen who was a custodian at his own high school—who cleaned urinals while his classmates looked on? He has traveled in some of the most expensive private jets and automobiles to some of the most exotic places on earth.

I share these details of my life with the utmost humility and give God all the glory. For it was by His hand and not my own that tremendous blessings have been part of my story. I also want you to see that it is possible to soar without limits when you seek God with all your heart then follow Him wherever He leads.

God used my own family, key individuals, and a host of other significant people to make it all possible. But ultimately, it was God's favor that enabled me to achieve success. And when a man's success comes from the hand of God, it always comes with a purpose.

He blesses us so we can be a blessing to

> *When one man, for whatever reason, has the opportunity to lead an extraordinary life, he has no right to keep it to himself.*
>
> ~ Jacques-Yves Cousteau, French undersea explorer

others. My story of rising from the ashes of hopeless poverty to the most famous stages of the world proves once again that with faith in God all things are possible.

In all honesty, the feelings I wrestled with as a young boy are to some degree many of the same emotional struggles that continue to challenge me today as a man. It's not like they have all magically disappeared just because I gave my heart to Jesus and achieved success.

As members of the human race, we are all broken in some way and will spend the rest of our lives trying to overcome our weaknesses. I am still a work in progress and there are more open-heart surgeries I must allow God to perform on me.

I have learned much on this incredible journey, and the revelatory truths have brought about magnificent changes in my vocational, personal, and spiritual life.

I am eternally grateful that God has shown me how to use my gifts and excel in spite of all my shortcomings and the varied circumstances that have tried to hold me back. In gratitude for His grace on my life, I have chosen to let Him use every experience in my life as a means to benefits others.

This is truly the purpose of our lives—to be used by God to fulfill His noble mission and to bring Him glory. Moving forward in faith—not being chained by our doubts, fears, inhibitions, and a checkered past—is one of the ways we bring Him glory.

Regardless of our lot in life, we all struggle with similar issues because they are the problems that are common to all mankind. But if we allow Him access to our lives, God will use absolutely every circumstance to tell a wonderful story of His transforming power. This, my friend, offers hope to all.

Our willingness to be used in this capacity will enable us to make a difference in the world, in a significant way that only we can. So, we shouldn't be afraid to let Him use the good, the bad, and the ugly to give depth, richness, and character to our lives.

We should never, ever count ourselves out of the race. With God on our side, absolutely nothing can disqualify us.

Imagine for a moment that long before you arrived on this planet, God set up a trust fund with your name on it. You could call it your personal potential account. There, in a special impenetrable vault, lies limitless potential with regard to the unique gifts and talents He gave you.

God's intention is for you to share those priceless treasures with the rest of the world by making regular withdrawals from that account throughout your life.

The unlimited potential God deposited inside of me is the same seed of unlimited potential He deposited inside of you. We are His children, made in His image, and therefore it is His seed of limitless potential that runs through our veins.

If only we could somehow fathom the excruciating detail that God put forth in designing every aspect of us as living and breathing creatures, then we would no longer wander the earth aimlessly. We would understand that we were created for a significant purpose.

Our Heavenly Father is the impassioned master sculptor who fashioned you out of the divine and unlimited resources of His eternal being. This potential to excel in your calling shows no partiality. It is the rightful destiny of every person on this planet to unearth this great potential and enjoy the gift of its expression.

We've all heard the adage: "They come from money." We commonly use that term to refer to people who are born into wealthy families and grow up with many resources at their disposal.

From heaven's perspective, we all come from money because God is the wealthiest Father in existence. He owns all the cattle on a thousand hills and we are His children, and therefore heirs to all He has.

In terms of potential, it's safe to say we all come from money. And in this particular sense, we are all equal heirs with an equal net worth.

Your ancestry, family background, race, and financial status have little to do with the incredible God-given potential for excellence that lies within you. Tapping into your potential only hinges on your desire to sift it out and ignite a passion in your heart to use it.

It would be a travesty to get to the end of your life only to realize that you withdrew a measly $10 from a proverbial personal account that had millions in it. But sadly, many people leave this earth with priceless assets that have gone untouched, undeveloped, and unclaimed.

In doing so, they fail to make the impact they might have. Countless opportunities to be a blessing to humanity are missed by those who take for granted the talents they've been given and the call that has been placed upon their lives.

The gifts and talents God has given you are irrevocable, which means He will never take them away from you—even if you choose not to develop them or serve Him with those talents.

The consequences for not using those assets, however, will result in a life of diminished value and unfulfilled purpose, and one that will leave you in a perpetual state of dissatisfaction.

Whether you see the value of what has been deposited into your personal potential account or not, you alone are responsible for discovering and using what you've been given.

All I know is that by the end of my life, I want my account to be empty, or even overdrawn, if possible.

Throughout all eternity, there has never been one exactly like you nor will there ever be. In fact, before you were born the idea of creating you was so innovative, so compelling and enthralling to God, that it began to consume Him. He meditated day and night on

> *It is a most mortifying reflection for a man to consider what he has done, compared to what he might have done.*
>
> ~ Samuel Johnson, English writer and poet

what you should be like and that brilliant image of you captivated His heart.

Then, finally, on one very magical day when the appointed time had come, He finished His marvelous creation and thusly brought it to life. And…BAM!…there you were in all your glorious magnificence!

You're an original creation, created for an original purpose in a very specific generation. Yet, God grants you the task of uncovering that purpose and allows you to choose whether you will engage your heart in the adventure He has prepared for you.

He brought you here to accomplish something profound while on this planet. And God must have felt the world would just not be complete without the presence of your distinguished company.

I would imagine He thought you were just too cool of a person to leave uncreated, so here you are with the rest of us on this planet, brought here to make your mark and make a difference.

> *Every beauty which is seen here by persons of perception resembles more than anything else that celestial source from which we all come.*
>
> ~ Michelangelo, Italian artist and architect

If you choose to believe in Him with all your heart, willfully aim to obey His commands and follow Him by faith, you will begin a never-ending adventure and the world will be forever changed by your very presence. Remember, God always uses people to fulfill His divine purposes and He wants to use you.

1

Life Principle #1

SURRENDER

Give Your Life to God

There are two kinds of people: those who say to God,
"Thy will be done," and those to whom God says,
"All right, then, have it your way."

~ C.S. Lewis, Irish author and Christian apologist

I had just finished a 10-year run playing drums behind some of the most popular recording artists of the decade. This good fortune enabled me to make a name for myself in one of the toughest industries in the world.

What's more, I managed to earn the respect of my musical heroes. Nothing meant more to me as a musician than to garner praise from those I once idolized and whose work I still admire.

The climb in my career was an arduous one—all the more reason I had such great appreciation for my achievement. I was on top of the world and enjoying the view.

Sadly, it didn't take long for my dream to crash, burn, and leave collateral damage. I had worked so hard to make my dreams reality and achieve the success so many only dream about. But I would soon discover that it's far easier to destroy something than it is to build it.

WHEN THE RED CARPET IS YANKED AWAY

I was a happily married man and very much in demand as a musician. I received an invitation to go on tour with French vocal superstar Vanessa Paradis, who at the time was France's equivalent of Beyoncé.

I accepted Vanessa's offer and was off to France. As the plane approached Charles De Gaulle Airport, the twinkling lights of Paris came into view and I could feel my spirit taking flight.

The tour commenced with two concert dates in the French-speaking Mauritius Islands. Those were followed by a week's vacation on a tropical island. It was paradise. We took helicopter rides through the lush mountain canyons and day trips to tranquil waterfalls. *Now, that's the way to start a tour,* I thought!

After arriving back in Paris, we performed for 30 straight nights to sold-out audiences at The Olympia, the legendary Parisian music hall founded in 1888. For the next several months, we embarked upon every province of France, hitting all the major and minor markets. On one of the tour dates, we even performed in an ancient amphitheater in the fairytale medieval city of Carcassonne.

It didn't take me long to figure out that when you're backing up one of France's biggest pop idols, the red carpet has a way of finding its way under your feet. Life felt grand and glamorous.

I had it all. Not only was I at the top vocationally and personally, I was sincerely flourishing spiritually, too.

A couple of years prior to the Paradis tour, I'd been working with four-time Grammy Award-winning singer/songwriter Lenny Kravitz. (He also played the character Cinna in *The Hunger Games* and *The Hunger Games: Catching Fire*.)

During one of the breaks from my tour with Lenny, I was visiting with dear friends and something profound happened.

My friends asked if I would let them pray for me. I said, "Sure, why not." As a result of their prayer, I felt the supernatural presence of God like never before. It was an epiphany, a spiritual awakening, and from that moment my life radically changed.

Even though I had asked Jesus into my heart to be my Lord and Savior when I was a young boy, I'd strayed and done my own thing for many years—until that day.

It was a profound turning point. I returned to the welcoming arms of my Heavenly Father and King to be engulfed by a love I had never known. I grew closer and closer to God with each passing day, and I pursued Him with all my heart, mind, and soul.

With God back at the helm, my career soaring and my personal life blossoming, I felt like all the key pieces had finally come together for me. I was living the dream.

That is, until I got home from the Paradis tour.

I arrived at Los Angeles International Airport on my birthday and was greeted by my wife. She took me out for lunch at a fun Mexican restaurant on the beach in Malibu.

There, shockingly, I was treated to the devastating news that she was having an affair. Not one of my better birthdays, for sure.

There are no words to express the depth of pain I felt. It wasn't enough that I'd been abandoned by my father as an infant; now I was being forsaken by the woman I had faithfully loved and served.

Even though God was back in the center of my life, the bomb that detonated on my heart tested everything in me—including my faith.

Maybe you've been in a similar situation. It's easy to have faith in God when you're prospering and there are no great challenges to overcome. But it's an altogether different story to stand strong in your faith when your world is eroding beneath you.

Faith is only made real as it endures a test. And I was about to be put to a test in the fullest measure.

I was tempted to get even with my wife after she confessed cheating on me. But as a follower of Jesus, I knew that would solve nothing and only bring about more regret. So I chose to honor my commitment to my wife—even if she didn't reciprocate. This took incredible restraint and much prayer. I would not have prevailed without God's help.

Despite my wife's less-than-noble character, I was willing to forgive her and reconcile our marriage. But no deal. She wanted a divorce. At the time, we owned two houses. We agreed that she would take the one in Seattle while I would keep the Los Angeles place.

My cherished wife moved out and moved on with a new boyfriend, new job, and new life. She nearly mortally wounded me financially too. I was practically penniless. My wife and her new love interest had blown through most of the money I sent home from the Paradis tour.

I was so distraught that I didn't have the emotional capacity or confidence to begin looking for a new gig. I crawled in a hole but couldn't stay in my bunker for long.

Shortly after my wife split, a major earthquake hit Los Angeles. The earthquake destroyed my home; my life literally came crashing down around me.

I lost just about every single thing I owned. I even had to sell the few possessions I had because I was homeless.

The church I was attending allowed me to host a garage sale. I couldn't believe that I had fallen so hard and fast. Here I was, selling my sequined stage clothes in the church parking lot to kids who were going to use them as Halloween costumes.

I found myself utterly dazed and confused. I was like a zombie riding the escalator of life to lower floors of emotional torment I never knew existed. I just kept clanging and banging and wondering when I would finally hit bottom.

After the yard sale, I was reduced to renting a bedroom from a sweet 90-year-old woman in Pasadena. I was grateful for the shelter but couldn't help wondering how I could have gone from gracing the covers of some of the most respected magazines in my industry to living in a tiny mauve-colored bedroom with a closet barely big enough to accommodate a winter coat.

It's not like I did something to bring all of this upon myself. I was not a stereotypical musician—the guy who boozes it up all night, sleeps all day, smokes dope, and cheats on his wife.

By contrast, I was a faithful husband and a hard-working man who had never been drunk or high in his life. I grew up in such dire straits that I never wanted to take part in behavior that could prevent me from taking flight.

I believed life was hard enough on its own without getting addicted to substances that could stifle my potential or destroy me. Money was so difficult to come by as a young boy that I could never fathom spending a dime of my hard-earned money on something that didn't bring a tangible benefit to my life.

But this was the reward for being a faithful man of God and making wise choices?

It felt like I went from being king of the castle to clown of the courtyard. During this agonizing time of my life, I learned that when a man hits rock bottom, his heart will be assailed beyond anything he has ever known. Absolutely every toxic emotion within the human spirit comes to the surface during a trial of this nature.

I was forced to grapple with pride, jealousy, self-pity, envy, bitterness, resentment, rage, anger, humiliation, sadness, sorrow, anguish, and a host of other morsels of madness.

These toxic emotions led me to the end of myself. I had no place to run…except back in the arms of my Jesus, the Son of God, where I would come to a full surrender.

At this time, I learned to cast all of my burdens, cares, and woes upon Him and left them at the foot of His throne. I would come to a new place in my relationship with God where I would have to trust Him not only for my future, but for my daily bread and every ounce of my provision.

> *Complete weakness and dependence will always be the occasion for the Spirit of God to manifest His power.*
>
> ~ Oswald Chambers, Scottish evangelist and author

The circumstances that led me to this place of trust were excruciating. But there also was a silver lining I couldn't see at the time. My freefall and rock-bottom splat would prove to be the best thing that ever happened to me. Much later I would even call it a gift.

THE COST OF GOING IT ALONE

It is only when we come to the end of ourselves that we can be ushered into the beginning of what God has for us. Among other things, surrendering brings with it an incredible sense of freedom. And it sets us up for future successes God already has planned.

Unfortunately, the word "surrender" gets a bad rap. Most often, we associate it with failure of some kind. And the stench of our pride makes it nearly impossible for us to view "surrender" as anything but defeat. That's simply not true.

In today's culture, winning has become so important that we absolutely dread the idea of conceding in any way. Some of us want to win so badly we're willing to obtain a victory at any cost. This obsession can be very dangerous because there's always a hidden cost to what we perceive as victory. A triumph in our career, for instance, sometimes can lead to disaster in our personal life.

The good news is there's a type of surrender that leads to authentic victory. It is a voluntary act and can only be invoked by exercising our own free will. It is the surrendering of one's heart, mind, and soul to the living God.

Surrender is the first and most important of the nine life principles presented in this book. Without it, we are left to our own devices to navigate the murky waters of life. Experience shows it seldom pans out well.

Despite their independent spirits, many

Everyone dies, but not everyone fully lives. Too many people are having a near-life experience.

~ Unknown

Hollywood stars and entertainment celebrities have been unable to attain fulfillment without God. An increasing number of highly successful entertainers who have self-destructed from drug-related issues reflect the reality of this epidemic of the soul.

Incredibly gifted actors such as Philip Seymour Hoffman, Heath Ledger, Chris Farley, and John Belushi needlessly left this world prematurely. Not to mention music legends the likes of Kurt Cobain, Whitney Houston, Jim Morrison, Janis Joplin, and Jimi Hendrix. All these lives tragically ended as a result of substance abuse of some kind or by suicide.

These are people who seemingly had everything. But fame, fortune, critical acclaim, sex, drugs, and even praise are not enough to satisfy the human soul. Despite partaking of all the delights this world has to offer, these creative geniuses were unable to satiate the deeper hunger within. Consequently, they turned elsewhere to fill that void. And like so many of us, they were looking in all the wrong places.

It's not just celebrities and other high-profile figures who are self-imploding these days. Countless people from all walks of life engage in the same self-destructive behavior for the same reasons. And, sadly, many suffer the same fate.

Today, there is a sense of spiritual desperation in the air. Like never before, people are craving a connection to something beyond what they can discern with their five senses. What they crave is a spiritual connection with the living God; they just don't know it.

That's because there's a vacant space in the soul of every male and female that God reserved for Him and Him alone. We are all lonely and longing for His presence. This emptiness cannot be filled with the lusts of the flesh and earthly pleasures. Any attempt to fill our lives with anything but God Himself will prove futile.

The pressures of this life can be unbearable at times. We live in a tough world. The only thing that will allow us to withstand the pressure is the grace of God on our lives.

> *He, Himself, is the fuel our spirits were designed to burn, or the food our spirits were designed to feed on. There is no other.*
>
> ~ C.S. Lewis, Irish author and Christian apologist

When God's presence surrounds someone's personal life and work, it brings a sense of peace and purpose that eludes those who do not have God in their lives.

This explains why so many people are dissatisfied in relationships and work that should bring them a deep sense of fulfillment. Remember, no form of work or personal connection will ever bring satisfaction to your soul if it is devoid of God's presence while you engage in it.

I emphasize this for you again, because it is the most important statement I will make in this book. *We were made by God, for God*, and only a close relationship with Him will bring us the spiritual connection we long for.

Throughout our lives, God's Spirit gently woos us to come to Him. He stands by, waiting ever so patiently for us to connect with Him. Please understand that God will never use tactics of coercion or manipulation to force us to make that happen. He wants us to want Him.

In the same way you couldn't possibly force someone to love you, neither will God force you to love and serve Him. Love can only reach the highest form of expression—surrender to God—through free will. Your willingness to surrender will come completely from your own heart or not at all.

THE "S" WORD

Unfortunately, some of you mistakenly think that giving your heart to Jesus means you'll have to sacrifice your dreams and desires—give up everything you cherish, sell everything you own, and live some mundane existence that is void of adventure.

Or you might think God wants you to go live in a third-world country as a missionary—forsaking the dreams you have for your future.

> *I am the vine; you are the branches. If you remain*
> *in me and I in you, you will bear much fruit;*
> *apart from me you can do nothing.*
> ~ Jesus, John 15:5

The most natural thing in the world is for us to want to run away from God and the call He has placed on our lives. It's the unknown. It's frightening. It's out of our control.

If you feel this way, then you're not alone. In fact, you're in very good company. There is a long line of notable VIPs of the faith who were just as terrified to answer God's call as perhaps you might be right now.

Consider Moses, one of the greatest and most well-known heroes of the Bible. When God called Moses to stand before Pharaoh, Moses wanted nothing to do with the assignment.

Moses would rather have been a valet, parking chariots for the Egyptians, than show his face in Pharaoh's court. Did you know that Moses begged God to send someone else?

Let's not forget that Jonah of the big fish story ran the other way when God called him to preach to the people of Nineveh. Jonah would end up in the belly of a whale before he finally conceded and did what God asked him to do. Talk about stubborn. Truthfully though, he sounds like so many of us.

But since God is God and He has purposes for all of us, He may very well ask you to do something you don't feel inspired or even qualified to do. In fact, He has been known to ask people to perform tasks in advance of supplying them with the corresponding desire to do so. That's OK. Really, it is.

The only thing that's important is to respond to the call with courage and move toward it by faith. In time, the desire will come. In the interim, God will often test your heart to see if you're going to place your trust in Him or in yourself.

If you place your confidence in Him, eventually God will come to your aid just as He did for those of the faith who have gone before us.

> *Too many people are thinking of security instead of opportunity. They seem to be more afraid of life than death.*
>
> ~ James F. Byrnes, American politician

Sometimes, God will plant the desire in your heart before actually calling you to the mission. You'll have a strong inclination to move in a certain direction long before you realize it was God who placed that desire within you in the first place.

In either case, He will always give you grace to match the level of the assignment and provide you with the means necessary to complete the assignment.

GIVING YOUR LIFE AWAY

In the movie *Machine Gun Preacher*, actor Gerard Butler plays real-life Sam Childers, the impassioned founder of Angels of East Africa Rescue Organization.

In the beginning of the film, we see Sam living a tempestuous life of violence and crime. From all-out bar brawls and sleeping with married women to selling narcotics and becoming an armed guard for drug dealers, Sam is up to his neck in trouble.

But eventually Sam has an epiphany and something significant happens to him—by the grace of God, he comes to a place of repentance. Sam changes his mind about the way he feels about sin and makes a decision to steer his life in the opposite direction.

It is not some robotic religious ritual. This kind of drastic transformation comes as a result of Sam's decision to receive Jesus Christ in his heart as his Lord and Savior.

This is now the second time in this chapter that I have mentioned someone receiving Jesus as Lord and Savior. The first mention was in reference to myself as a young boy.

I realize that although most of you have probably heard the name of Jesus at some point in your life, some of you may not know exactly who He is and what His claims were.

So I thought it would be important to have a basic understanding of Jesus before moving on. I've given a description below of who Jesus is titled "Who Is Jesus?". I encourage you to read it before getting back to the story.

WHO IS JESUS?

Jesus is the Son of God. He was born miraculously of a virgin and lived as a boy then man among the Jewish people some 2,000 years ago. Jesus allowed himself to be crucified on a cross and became the sacrifice that God demanded in payment for the sins of mankind.

He was buried but conquered death, hell, and the grave by coming back to life on the third day. Jesus lives in heaven with God, our Father, and reigns at His right hand.

Jesus is our advocate. Believing in Him and trusting our lives to Jesus by faith puts us in right standing with God, and grants us eternal life in heaven and access to a more abundant life here on earth.

For God so loved the world that he gave his one and
only Son, that whoever believes in him shall
not perish but have eternal life.
For God did not send his Son into the world to condemn
the world but to save the world through him.
~ John 3:16-17

His resurrection from the dead is what separates Jesus from every other religious figure in history. Jesus is the only one who ever came back to life. He later ascended into heaven. Jesus is alive today and will be forevermore.

All authority over heaven and earth has been given to Jesus by God. Each of us will stand before Jesus to give an account of our lives after we die. The Bible tells us that Jesus will return to this earth one day. And upon His return, every knee will bow and every tongue will confess that Jesus Christ is Lord.

He is referred to in the Bible as the Son of God, the King of kings, the Lord of lords, and the Lamb of God who took away the sins of the world. His claims were unlike any in the history of the world. Jesus claimed to be the Son of God and proved it with signs, wonders, miracles, and His eventual resurrection.

Jesus loves you and has plans to give you hope and a future. He wants to be sure you live eternally in heaven with Him.

I am the way and the truth and the life.
No one comes to the Father except through me.
~ Jesus, John 14:6

The Spirit of God always woos us to Himself. The question is, will we respond to that gentle whisper? Sometimes we lose our way. And since we're given the freedom to make our own choices, we often make the wrong ones.

Fortunately, God's house is never closed and the palace gates will open with just the slightest nudge from us. Our Heavenly Father welcomes every prodigal son and daughter home into the safety of His arms, and grants us mercy and forgiveness as well as restoration of our souls.

That's how it worked for the Machine Gun Preacher. As Sam gains access to his Savior's never-ending grace, slowly, a new man begins to emerge—a man who senses a divine destiny ahead and decides to start following God's voice. With God's help, Sam begins to rebuild his life and finds honest work using his natural talent for building. He eventually gets married and starts his own construction company.

Through a church-sponsored mission trip, God leads Sam from his home in Pennsylvania to the village of Yei in Southern Sudan. At the time, the African nation is in the midst of the Second Sudanese War. There, Sam uses his carpentry skills to help repair huts damaged by the war.

While on this life-changing trip, Sam comes across the scattered body of a child who was dismembered by a land mine. Sam vows to God that he will do all he can to help the people of Southern Sudan.

> *Have plenty of courage. God is stronger than the devil. We are on the winning side.*
>
> ~ John Chapman, British theologian

Sam's powerful testimony challenges us on many levels. It makes us wonder what kind of adventure God would have for us if we choose to surrender to Him.

Gerard Butler was quoted as saying of Sam Childers, "The man has experienced more than most people would in ten lifetimes."

To know God intimately requires you to surrender your life and plans to Him so He can reroute the GPS and lead you toward the divine path He has prepared for you.

Surrendering will be the gateway to your greatest revelations, miracles, and victories. It will also provide you with unique opportunities to impact the world in the most personal and radical ways.

Don't stand on the riverbank seeking safety. Jump in and join God for some white-water adventures. I promise a most amazing revelation. You'll see that in spite of the perceived danger, you'll actually be swimming with the current instead of against it.

GOD'S GIFTS TO YOU

One of the primary reasons so few people surrender to God is because the enemy (yep, Satan is real, even if you've been told otherwise) fools them into believing God will take something from them. The opposite is true.

God wants to *give* you something—more than you can ask or imagine. He wants to shower you with expressions of His love by giving you vision, purpose, peace, joy, healing, and hope. He wants to restore, revitalize, and redirect you.

If He wants to take anything away from you, it will be what most of us would gladly give away in a heartbeat—emptiness, pain, fear, anxiety, distress, sickness, disease, anguish, pressure, and emotions that are detrimental to you.

> *Since that day, there is nothing anyone could ever say to convince me that one person cannot change a nation. One person can do unbelievable things. All it takes is that one person who's willing to risk everything to make it happen.*
>
> ~ Sam Childers, founder of Angels of East Africa Rescue Organization

What good earthly father wouldn't take a dangerous weapon or toxic poison out of the hands of his child? When Sam Childers offered his life in service to God, the Lord helped remove the desire for evil and corruption that would have eventually destroyed Sam. God replaced it with the desire to do good works, which gave Sam new meaning to his life.

If God wants to rid you of anything, it will be bad habits, addictions, wrong ideologies, wayward philosophies, and unhealthy attitudes that eventually will destroy you.

Naturally, life will present you with many difficult decisions. Eyes that are not submitted to God are blind eyes, and they cannot see what needs to be seen to survive and thrive.

Little did Sam Childers know the profound impact he would have on the children of Southern Sudan when he surrendered his life to Jesus Christ. With God's favor, direction, and protection, Sam built an orphanage and then began to lead armed missions to rescue children who were victims of the war.

It didn't take long for the tales of his noble exploits to spread, and soon the local villagers called him the Machine Gun Preacher. Today, the orphanage is the largest in Southern Sudan and has fed and housed more than 1,000 children.

YOUR BEST DAYS ARE AHEAD

There was no way I could have known back when my life fell apart how God would later orchestrate my restoration. Eventually, I would discover that my best days were not behind me as I had thought. They were actually just up ahead in the future.

During that time of my greatest trials, I made the decision to honor God no matter what happened to me and stay submitted to Him and Him alone. I also made a vow to God that after my divorce from my ex-wife was final I would remain celibate until I married again—and I didn't know if that would ever happen.

It's fascinating to see how the lessons we need today are staring at us from the pages of the Bible.

Did you know that one of the few times King David lost a battle on behalf of the Israelites was when he failed to consult God on a matter? He made a decision to go to battle without inquiring of the Lord, and it cost him dearly.

After my failed marriage experience, I decided that I would consult God on absolutely every important decision of my life—and even the minor ones too.

God tested me, sure. But how can loyalty be proven genuine without a test? I also tested God during that time, and He had no problem passing my test. I wanted to see if God would really reward a man who was willing to give up everything to follow Him.

I made my relationship with God my top priority and did my best to follow His commands and respond in obedience to His call on my life.

God is a God of His word. Graciously, He would restore all that was taken from me and I would eventually take flight again. This time I would soar to even higher heights and be showered with favor I could not earn. He took me places I would not dare imagine. And like a child, I was in awe through it all.

> *The blessing of the Lord makes a person rich,*
> *and he adds no sorrow with it.*
> ~ Proverbs 10:22 (NLT)

For starters, there would be bigger and better gigs, nicer homes than the one smashed by the earthquake, numerous industry awards and recognition as a musician, author, educator, and speaker.

I once again was on the covers of prestigious magazines and made television appearances around the world. I've even gone to the White House.

A long list of other dreams that were hiding deep in my heart since childhood have been fulfilled too. You'll read about some of them in upcoming chapters.

God has blessed me tremendously in my vocation, and He has given a deep sense of meaning and purpose to all that I've undertaken. But I don't share any of this to brag in any way. I boast only in what God has done and in the power of His mighty hand. It is all for His glory.

I also share this to remind you that God is able to do what He said He would do, and to encourage you to pursue Him with all your heart.

As I stayed in a place of submission, God restored mine completely. But God didn't stop with restoration. He rewarded me, and it has been truly wonderful.

More important than anything that has transpired in my career, God blessed me in a personally intimate way with a precious woman of God. Her name is Renee, and she is the wife I trusted God would bring me.

His grace and faithfulness have been upon our lives since the day He first presented Renee to me. I kept my end of the bargain and so did God. He's been the invisible third partner of this marriage and kept us united now for 20 years and counting!

In addition, God gave us two incredible children whom I love more than anything in this world. They have filled my heart with unspeakable joy and added a dimension to my life that I cannot articulate in words.

Of course, none of this came without a battle, extremely hard work, and the continual testing of my faith. Yet every aspect of my life has experienced godly increase since the time I hit rock bottom. He has increased my platform and the impact I've been able to have in this world. God's faithfulness continues to astound me.

I am closer to God now than I have ever been. I hope to be even closer with the dawning of each new day. God is definitely great, and I am only able to share this story with you because God is faithful!

> *Great faith is the product of great fights. Great testimonies are the outcome of great tests. Great triumphs can only come out of great trials.*
>
> ~ Smith Wigglesworth, British evangelist and author

SURRENDER: A QUICK SUMMARY

- God loves you and created you to have fellowship with Him.
- God has a plan and purpose for your life.
- Surrendering to God allows you access to that divine plan.
- God's plan for you is better than anything you can plan for yourself.
- Giving your heart to Jesus gives Him permission to intervene, act on your behalf, and assure you of eternal life with Him in heaven.
- Surrendering your heart to God will always be an act of will.

Your Personal Prayer

Dear God,
I willingly surrender my life to You, and I ask You, Lord Jesus, to come into my heart and lead me by Your Spirit to all that You have planned and purposed for me in this life. I admit that I am a sinner, and I am in need of Your forgiveness. Today by faith, I receive Your gift of eternal life, Your everlasting love, and Your promises for my future. Amen.

2

DISCOVER
Identify Your Gifts And Talents

*Don't ask what the world needs. Ask what makes you
come alive, and go do it. Because what the world
needs is people who have come alive.*

~ Howard Thurman, American author and theologian

My first step toward becoming a professional drummer started quite humbly in fourth grade. It all began with a talent show at Jerome Prairie Elementary in Grants Pass, Oregon.

I had no sticks, no drums, and no cymbals. I owned absolutely no drumming equipment whatsoever. All I had was this incredible desire to play and a really big heart. I had no choice but to improvise. I ended up playing with my hands on a huge, empty Maytag refrigerator box.

We played the Elvis Presley arrangement of *I've Never Been to Spain*. And once I felt the rhythms vibrating on that beat-up cardboard, I knew I would never be the same. From the onset of that very special moment, I wanted desperately to be part of the school band and play the drums.

But year after excruciatingly disappointing year, I was told there were too many drummers. Mr. Erickson, the band director, told me that I would have to choose another instrument if I wanted to participate in the program. Finally, in the seventh grade, I was in…playing the trumpet.

I really had no passion for the instrument but was inspired briefly when my mother reminded me that the trumpet was always the lead voice in all of those triumphant soundtracks from movies I really enjoyed. Epics such as *Spartacus*, *Ben-Hur*, *Rocky*, and the films of the James Bond series featured those blazing high notes that I imagined myself belting out. Even the Beatles' classic *All You Need Is Love* featured some really cool trumpet parts, so I thought how bad could this be?

My performance on the trumpet proved bad, embarrassingly bad. I knew I needed some serious instruction to play even beginner music on the trumpet.

At the start of my first semester, Mr. Erickson sat me in a practice room all by myself, handed me the book *John Kinyon's Basic Training Course for Trumpet Book 1* and said, "Here, learn the trumpet," and then proceeded to close the door on his way out.

Unbelievable as it may sound, he didn't teach me a single thing about how to play the instrument. Mr. Erickson never even peeked his head in throughout the semester to see how—or if—I was progressing. If he had, he would have found that I made absolutely no progress at all.

There I sat for two long semesters, frustrated with the trumpet and bored out of my mind. Rather than waste away in my cell, I decided I would read *The Adventures of Huckleberry Finn*. It was a far better read than my band method book, which looked like Braille to me.

One day toward the end of that school year, Mr. Erickson finally decided to call me out of my dungeon to unleash his secret prodigy on the rest of the ensemble.

It was an absolutely terrifying experience because I couldn't read a lick of the music and I knew that despite my faithfulness to Mark Twain, he wouldn't be coming to my aid anytime soon.

I could feel my heart racing and my hands starting to get clammy in anticipation of my moment of dreadful, nauseating truth. Beads of sweat slowly dripped down over my brows and into my eyes as the first inkling of sound began to protrude from the mouthpiece.

With the stinging, salty perspiration impairing my vision, I kept my eyes closed and felt more like Ray Charles than trumpet virtuoso Maynard Ferguson.

One major problem here. I've never met anyone or heard of anyone who can attempt to read music with his or her eyes closed. That was OK though. I really didn't want to watch the audience watching me.

I really, really didn't want anyone else in the band staring at me. If you've ever been in seventh grade, you know how devastating peer pressure can be. Being dissed by 12- and 13-year-olds can be downright paralyzing for a kid who doesn't have a clue what he's supposed to do in such a high-stakes situation.

TAAADAAAA!...There it was in all its triumphant, brassy, loud glory. A sound that commanded attention. Unfortunately, my trumpet blast failed to garner the kind of attention I had hoped.

My new bandmates stared at me in utter amazement. The look on their faces said, "What the heck is that sound? It ain't music, that's for sure."

Flight of the Bumblebee it was not. I had released a sharp, piercing so-called note that could send a pack of wild hyenas running for cover. Actually, it felt more like the soundtrack to *Titanic*. I sank very quickly into my chair, wishing I possessed invisible powers.

It was a traumatizing experience to say the least. That musical cataclysm would haunt me for a long time and undermine my confidence. How could I ever really become a musician? What was I thinking?

To everyone's relief, that was my last day in junior high band and it definitely didn't end on a high note. My dream of playing the drums seemed a million miles away at that point. And despite my annual attempts to reenter the school band program as a drummer, it wouldn't be until my sophomore year in high school that I was finally able to start my formal percussion studies.

Yet somehow back on that fateful day of the Maytag box-banging talent show in fourth grade, I stumbled upon one of the gifts God had given me.

> *Catch on fire with enthusiasm and people will come for miles to watch you burn.*
>
> ~ Charles Wesley, English leader of the Methodist movement and hymn writer

An intense desire to do something with it burned in my heart from that day forward. Despite my temporary departure from music after the agonizing trumpet fiasco, every time I thought of playing the drums it electrified my spirit and gave my soul a magnetic charge.

A PRAYER TO DISCOVER YOUR GIFTING AND TALENTS

After making the most important decision you'll ever make—surrendering your life to Jesus Christ—the next step toward achieving personal success is to discover the unique gifts and talents God has given you.

This life principle No. 2 is full of exciting possibilities. And it involves a process that will require your commitment to patience and diligence.

Since God took the time to create you and me and everyone else as uniquely individual, it's safe to assume He wants us to do something big with the unique abilities He bestowed upon us.

Far and away, the absolute best way to discover your gifts and talents and determine how God wants you to use them is to *ask* Him.

We do this by respectfully coming before God in prayer. By the way, there is no secret formula for praying. It is a conversation you initiate with the Creator of the Universe who also is your Heavenly Father.

God cares more deeply for you than you can imagine. He wants to talk with you. Sometimes it's hard for us to accept that God really looks upon us as His children and wants what's best for us. But trust me, He does.

Spend time alone with God. When you block off device-free and distraction-free time during your day to be with God, you can be sure it will be worth it.

Seek Him and He will be found. It might seem a little strange at first, but it's easy to experience God's presence. You'll know it by the peace you feel when praying. Ask Him to provide direction on how to recognize your gifts and talents.

If God sees your earnest desire to make use of your skills for His glory and for the betterment of His people, then you can be confident He will confirm the direction you are to take. Still, it will be a walk of faith.

Did you know that more than anything, it is faith that moves the heart of God? When He sees you demonstrate it in some way as you're discovering your abilities and how to use them, God is greatly pleased.

A man from the Old Testament of the Bible who exemplified great faith was Joseph, the highly-favored son of Jacob who lived an unbelievable life of purpose and success. You wouldn't have believed it, though, from the way it started out.

As a young boy, Joseph was deeply resented by his 11 brothers. They were so jealous of Joseph that they sold him as a slave and told their father he was killed by wild animals.

Along the way, Joseph became a servant-slave for a high-ranking Egyptian official named Potiphar. Discovering and developing his gifts for leadership and administration eventually led Joseph to become head of Potiphar's estate. Life was going quite well until Potiphar's wife falsely accused Joseph of attempted rape.

Although Joseph was innocent and demonstrated absolute loyalty to Potiphar, he was sent to prison for years. Being a man of strong faith and uncompromising conviction, Joseph chose to trust God and make the best of a terrible and unjust situation.

Through Joseph's close relationship with God, he was able to recognize and develop the many gifts and talents God gave him. And

Joseph was faithful to serve God and others with each of them—even in prison.

God also gave Joseph the ability to interpret dreams, and this spiritual gift led him to explain a disturbing dream of the Pharaoh of Egypt. As a result, Joseph was released from prison and eventually ascended to second in command of Egypt—behind only Pharaoh himself.

The story concludes with Joseph saving the people of Egypt from a devastating famine, reconciling with his brothers, bringing his father's extended family to live peacefully next to Egypt, and guaranteeing that his own family lineage would continue. Eventually, Jesus Christ, the Savior of the world, would come from that lineage.

Faith is the invisible currency of heaven, and God will always honor those who put their faith in Him. If you have strong faith, you can accomplish far more with a single talent than a person with many talents who lacks faith.

In Romans 12:3, the Bible tells us "God has given every man a measure of faith." Faith itself is a free gift that God bestows upon you. It too can be compared to a seed. If you nurture and protect your faith, eventually it will yield a harvest.

Whether you choose to place your faith in God or yourself is entirely up to you. Faith in yourself is a dangerous high-wire act. As you've already read, life without God will leave a tremendous void in your soul that no amount of success and achievement will be able to fill.

A relationship with God based on faith brings with it a tremendous amount of spiritual assets that are unavailable to those whose faith is merely in themselves and their abilities.

Your personal relationship with the Creator will lead to discovery of your gifts and talents as well as fulfillment of His purposes for your life. All of that will enable you to flourish personally, spiritually, and vocationally.

Ready for some excitement? Discovering your God-given abilities also requires a willingness to take risks. There is no faith where there is no risk. It doesn't exist. You must be willing to take a fall before you can take a bow.

CAN YOU HANDLE THE TRUTH?

Progress always involves risks. You can't steal second and keep your foot on first.

~ Robert Quillen, American journalist and humorist

Another effective way to determine where you naturally excel is by enlisting the perspective of those you feel would be honest with you. This can be one of your teachers, a mentor, family member, or a trusted friend whose opinion you value.

Without exception, we all have a blind spot when it comes to being able to accurately evaluate ourselves. Making these kinds of vital inquiries can be extremely beneficial when trying to assess your potential in a specific area.

To do this, you must communicate a willingness to receive the truth with humility. If those you enlist for feedback sense you can't handle the truth, they may not be inclined to give you their honest assessment. You must remain open to hearing their responses and giving thoughtful consideration to what you hear.

It's not that you should allow any single opinion to have the final say in your life. But honestly, if 19 of 20 trusted sources tell you they don't believe you possess a particular talent, they might be right. Perhaps you don't have that talent—or maybe you do, but no one can see it emerging just yet.

Whatever the truth may be, the Bible asserts there is wisdom in the multitude of counsel. If you want to be wise, seek out the multitude for that counsel and then pray God would help you decipher the truth for yourself.

As these revelations about your unique abilities come to you, it's important for you to look for the common thread in all of them. At times, the answer to what you're gifted at is as simple as what consistently comes naturally to you.

Other times, there will be certain tasks you undertake that—even with massive amounts of effort—will still yield only mediocre results. These clues can help you identify skills and instincts that you innately display.

The apostle Paul confirmed that God graced each of us with particular gifts and talents for specific purposes. The main thing he emphasized was to use those gifts and talents, whatever they are, to the best of our ability in service to God and others.

In his grace, God has given us different gifts for doing certain things well. So if God has given you the ability to prophesy, speak out with as much faith as God has given you. If your gift is serving others, serve them well. If you are a teacher, teach well. If your gift is to encourage others, be encouraging. If it is giving, give generously. If God has given you leadership ability, take the responsibility seriously. And if you have a gift for showing kindness to others, do it gladly.
~ Romans 12:6-8

When asking God for confirmation of your gifts and talents, you must keep your spirit open and be alert because God communicates in many ways.

He can send a message directly to your heart or mind. He can choose to convey His response through other people. He may even present the answer in the form of a vision or dream.

And as many people can testify, God has been known to get our attention through thwarted plans and plain old frustration.

Sometimes, God will allow you to get so fed up with your present circumstances that you finally muster enough courage to pursue the thing you should have gone after in the first place. I call this a God-inspired discontentedness.

I don't believe God will allow you to ever feel truly satisfied as long as you're not exercising the gifts He gave you.

> *Discontent is the first necessity of progress.*
>
> ~ Thomas Edison, American inventor and businessman

Even if you can somehow achieve a level of success through efforts that are independent of Him, those achievements will be unable to provide a genuine sense of purpose if they remain outside your divine calling.

Another great exercise for the purpose of discovery is to go inward. Ask yourself, "When do I feel most alive?" Chances are, that activity is linked to your gifts and purpose.

Sometimes, the thing you're destined to do is right under your nose and so obvious that you can easily miss it. What do you dream about that makes you feel inspired and excited? That could be God talking to you.

Personally, I feel most alive when I'm drumming, speaking, writing, teaching, mentoring, and encouraging. When I am immersed in any of these activities, I feel an incredible sense of well-being.

As I engage in this work, an unbridled passion and inner joy just oozes out of me naturally. That's because God wired me to respond in that manner to those forms of expression.

> *The place where God calls you is where your deep gladness and the world's hunger meet.*
>
> ~ Frederick Buechner, American writer and theologian

You too will experience the same feeling when you discover the activities that touch your spirit unlike anything else. When you find them, they will set your heart on fire and help catapult you toward your purpose.

Keep in mind there will be various tasks to accomplish throughout the many stages of life. Each of us has been divinely equipped with a variety of gifts to impact the world.

Different gifts will be developed and deployed at different seasons for altogether different reasons. If you cooperate with God, He will most certainly make use of all your gifts to get the job done.

DEVELOPING YOUR PASSION

As a drummer entrenched in the world of rock and roll, I've been fortunate to literally travel the globe as part of my profession. Countless trips to a wide range of fascinating places have afforded me the opportunity to rub shoulders with many giants of accomplishment.

On one such trip, I had the distinct pleasure of sitting next to legendary tennis champion Serena Williams. We met on a flight from Paris to Rome while I was playing on a European tour with Lenny Kravitz.

I found Serena to be an exuberant woman and quite engaging. We chatted throughout the flight and laughed quite a bit as well. It was a memorable flight, indeed. But the one surprising fact I have never forgotten is when Serena told me she started playing tennis at the age of 4.

I thought to myself, "Well, there you go then; that explains everything." I also wondered how much better of a drummer I could have been if I started playing at age 4 instead of 16.

> *Luck has nothing to do with it, because I have spent many, many hours, countless hours, on the court working for my one moment in time, not knowing when it would come.*
>
> ~ Serena Williams

There are some people who display an innate gifting at a very early age and are fortunate enough to be encouraged to develop it from the start.

Such was the case for Serena Williams and her sister Venus, when their parents led them into the sport of tennis before they were old enough to attend kindergarten. Both worked diligently on developing their talents, and they turned out to be world champions.

Other early bloomers who went on to achieve success? Wolfgang

Amadeus Mozart began showing signs of musical brilliance at the age of 3, and was composing music when he was 5 years old.

Golf champion Tiger Woods was in a class of his own as a child, and is as an adult. I remember seeing Tiger in his first television appearance on the *Mike Douglas Show* in 1978. The toddling 2-year-old putted against comedian Bob Hope. Tiger demonstrated the most incredible precision with a golf club of any child in the world. It was truly a wonder to behold.

> *As a kid I might have been psycho, I guess. I used to throw golf balls in the trees and try and somehow make par from them. I thought it was fun.*
>
> ~ Tiger Woods

And just as there are early bloomers, there are those who blossom later in life. Late bloomers are those among us who don't discover their true talents until later than expected. But you just have to love those people who refuse to let what others say about their potential define or limit them.

These courageous individuals inspire me by their refusal to be held to some imaginary time line that dictates when one is supposed to blossom. Age does not disqualify us from the race because with God all things are possible.

Take a look at football quarterback Kurt Warner. Kurt didn't enter the NFL until he was 28, which was supposedly well past an athlete's prime for that sport. Nevertheless, he went on to become a two-time MVP and Super Bowl champion.

Scottish singing sensation Susan Boyle was virtually unknown until she sang *I Dreamed a Dream* from *Les Miserables* on the reality television program *Britain's Got Talent*. She was 48 at the time.

One of my favorite stories of a man who refused to let his age stand in the way of his lifelong dream is that of Burt Munro, the New Zealand-born motorcycle racer.

Burt was age 68 when he rode a 47-year-old motorcycle to set the

> *You are never too old to set another goal or to dream a new dream.*
>
> ~ C.S. Lewis, Irish author and Christian apologist

> *Nothing splendid has ever been achieved except by those who dared to believe that something inside them was superior to circumstance.*
>
> ~ Bruce Barton, American author and politician

land-speed record at Bonneville Salt Flats in Utah. The record still stands. Burt's truly inspiring story can be seen in the movie *The World's Fastest Indian*.

My point in sharing these anecdotes is to remind you that it doesn't matter when you discover your talents or develop a passion for something.

It makes no difference whether you're young, middle age, advancing in years, or close to knocking on heaven's door. What's important is that you find the courage to discover what you've been given and then use it to make a quantifiable difference on this planet while you're still alive to do it.

TOWARD THE AHA MOMENT

As you focus on discovering your natural talents, be prepared to accept that they may not be something you think is all that special. They might not even be something you truly like at first.

But eventually, if you embrace what you have, a passion for using those gifts will grow as well as an appreciation for them. You can only conclude that God has His divine reasons for choosing the gifts and abilities you now possess. And He has a definite purpose behind them.

If you are faithful to develop those talents and feed those passions, you can be sure you will experience a heavenly contentment that comes as a result of your willingness to cooperate.

It's not imperative that you fully understand the purpose of your unique gifts in advance before deciding to make use of them.

In fact, God's greatest desire is that you rely on Him to lead you through the process and trust that what He's given you to work with is just as significant as anyone else's talent.

We've all watched great performances of renowned athletes, actors, and musicians excelling at their craft. After witnessing such inspiring moments, you'll often hear people make comments such as, "Wow, so and so is incredibly talented," or "Man, they've been touched by God."

As obvious as that may be, what's not so obvious is the fact that we're all talented, gifted, and touched by God. Sadly, due to a lack of vision on our part, we often cast aside our own abilities and in doing so place self-imposed limits on our potential by our own neglect.

We simply must come to terms with the fact that we can't all be eyes, ears, and noses. God made every body part and organ for a specific purpose. We need all of them for the human body to function as a whole.

Someone has to play the part of a leg, arm, heart, brain, muscles, bones, and tendons. In that same manner, the world needs every gift God gave to man in order for society to function as a whole, because we're all a part of that vast design.

> *One principle reason why men are so often useless is that they neglect their own profession or calling and divide and shift their attention among a multitude of objects and pursuits.*
>
> ~ Nathanael Emmons, American theologian

Without all of the individual and varied forms of creative expression we possess as human beings, the world would be a terribly inefficient and boring place. Each of us serves a specific function to the overall body in a personal way, and one that our world cannot do without.

So rather than resist your natural gifting, you would be wise to embrace it so you can run the race with the talent you've been given. This is truly the key to your flourishing.

There would be no way I could have known on the day of that talent

> *If a man does not keep pace with his companions, perhaps it is because he hears a different drummer. Let him step to the music he hears, however measured or far away.*
>
> ~ Henry David Thoreau, American author and philosopher

show back in the fourth grade the incredible doors God would open for me later in life and the amazing people I would have the privilege of knowing.

Through God's grace and favor—and my willingness to discover my talents, work hard, and walk in faith—He made a glorious way for my gift to shine before millions around the world.

> *A man's gift makes room for him and brings him before great men.*
> ~ Proverbs 18:16 (NKJV)

I would go from pounding on a beat-up cardboard box with my hands to playing the finest drums and cymbals money could buy at the most prestigious venues in the world.

Eventually, I would even be granted the privilege of creating signature drumming products that bore my name for which I would receive royalties. This amazed me more than anyone else. All I can do is give glory to God and reaffirm through my personal testimony that, once again, with God all things are possible.

Remember, there is no single method for the unveiling and uncovering of the gifts and talents God gives you. Neither is there an exact predestined time for their discovery, because any time is a good time to find a treasure chest full of gold.

This discovery process is not a one-time event, but rather an ongoing journey throughout your life.

Sometimes you have to experiment with a variety of activities before eventually stumbling upon the area you are most enthused about.

If you have yet to discover what you are passionate about, then try volunteering for something that at least piques your interest to see if there is a love connection for that type of work.

The more you investigate different activities, types of work, and service, the more you can be assured that God will lead you to that "aha" moment that captivates your heart. He wants you to find it for sure. You just have to press in hard until it surfaces.

Even when you're uncertain about what to pursue, you must still make the first move. Choose to get involved and then be willing to take risks. As you display that courage, God will honor your faith by illuminating your path with a glorious light.

Your commitment to unearth the personal treasures you possess puts your faith into action and proves to God that you're serious about making your mark on this world.

It is only after discovering within yourself a talent or passion that you can begin to dream about how you might use it. Dreaming is the next life principle you must apply to reach your potential.

> *Twenty years from now, you will be more disappointed by the things that you didn't do than the ones you did do. So throw off the bowlines. Sail away from the safe harbor. Catch the trade winds in your sails. Explore. Dream. Discover.*
>
> ~ H. Jackson Brown Jr., American author

DISCOVER: A QUICK SUMMARY

- God graciously gave you gifts and talents to impact the world.
- God wants you to discover your gifts and talents, and He grants you the task of uncovering them.
- God wants you to embrace the gifts He gave you and use them to serve Him and His people. God wants you to make an indelible mark on this planet.

- Discovering your gifts and talents is a process that takes courage and commitment.
- It is never too early or too late to discover your gifts, talents, and passions.

Your Personal Prayer

Dear God,
I earnestly ask You to reveal to me the great gifts that You have deposited in me so I might better understand the purpose for which I was made. Please give me spiritual revelation and insight into these matters of great importance so I might be a vessel of honor that glorifies You in all I do. Amen.

3

DREAM

Uncover Your Purpose

Some of us let our dreams die, but others nourish and
protect them, nurse them through bad days till they bring
them to sunshine and light, which always come to those
who sincerely believe that their dreams will come true.

~ Woodrow Wilson, 28th president of the United States

Not long after I officially started playing drums, I wrote down on a piece of notebook paper that I wanted to write a book on rhythm and blues drummers. The crazy thing was that I was only 16 at the time and knew next to nothing about the topic. I really had nothing on which to base the rationale.

Yet I was somehow drawn to the idea, and it became a secret desire of my heart. And while I didn't realize it at the time, I was actually *dreaming* with God and learning how to cast a vision for my future.

Fast-forward 20 years to the writing of my first book—*The Commandments of R&B Drumming: A Comprehensive Guide to Soul, Funk and Hip Hop*. Amazingly, the book was voted the best educational book of 2000 by many top drum industry magazine readers' polls. It became a bestseller in the field and opened many doors around the world for me as a music educator.

Several years after being on the market, it was listed as one of the "25 Timeless Drum Books" by *Modern Drummer* magazine, the premiere industry publication.

What a wild experience. I suddenly found myself in the company of a small group of legendary authors of the most classic drum books ever written. Some of those titles came out as early as 1935, and most of them I studied out of myself in my developmental years.

It seemed impossible to compete with books that were so deeply ingrained in the fabric of the worldwide drumming community. Yet somehow, the outrageous dream God had given me as a teenager came to pass.

I still marvel at what the Lord was able to do through me. I have never doubted the power of dreams and vision. And I've always believed that if God's favor is upon me, then anything is possible.

The funny thing was, I had forgotten writing out such a lofty goal until long after the book's success. Luckily for me, on one of those massive spring-cleaning weekends, I stumbled upon an old school folder where I discovered that original piece of notebook paper and other treasures.

As I sifted through those hand-written documents like an archaeologist uncovering the Dead Sea Scrolls, I felt truly enlightened. Those writings clearly told a story from long ago.

In that folder were many such visions, which expressed exactly what was in a young man's heart and what he dreamed about. Surprisingly, I had the sense to journal them.

> *All you need in this life is ignorance and confidence, and then success is sure.*
>
> ~ Mark Twain, American author and humorist

And I was just ignorant enough to believe I could achieve them. Like a fossil embedded in the side of a mountain, those writings marked in time and accurately traced the origin of some of my first dreams. It was a fascinating discovery.

POWER OF VISION

Every great vision that God imparts to you He gives in the form of a dream that takes place in your heart, mind, and soul. Life principle No. 2 was discovering the gifts and talents God gave you. As you uncover those unique abilities, you can begin implementing life principle No. 3, which is to dream about how you might use them.

God's dreams for you have present-day purpose as well as eternal implications. In His faithfulness, God has endowed you with the necessary potential and provided you with the full capacity to live out those dreams. But only the brave and the bold will pursue these dreams to completion.

Have you ever taken the time to realize that the day you arrived on this planet those dreams were secretly hidden in your infant heart? It's astounding! Dreams from God have always been lodged deep inside of you, waiting to be uncovered.

Contrary to what you might think, God is not hiding His dreams from you. In actuality, He is hiding them *for* you to discover and take pleasure in. Dreams take time to uncover and unfold, but this is where the great adventure lies.

Without a dream to pursue, life quickly becomes uninspiring, monotonous, and uneventful at best. Until the ignition of your heart is turned on by a divine vision worth pursuing, your life remains in a vast wasteland of the mundane.

Your personal, spiritual, and vocational fulfillment is linked to the pursuit of your dreams because they are linked to God's purpose for your life.

Be careful, though, to not pursue false dreams; they will be disappointingly dissatisfying because it is not what God purposed you to do.

As is necessary for the building of any structure, there is a logical progression that must take place for any dream to be realized. That process requires the diligence of mapping out the vision on paper.

An interesting study on goal setting conducted by Gail Matthews, PhD, a psychology professor at Dominican University in California, confirmed the benefits of writing out your goals. The study revealed that people are 42 percent more likely to achieve their goals by writing them out.

Since I can personally attest to the power of writing out visions and dreams, the findings of this study didn't surprise me at all. If you haven't been doing so already, I certainly hope this information encourages you to start the process for yourself.

Just so we're clear, writing out goals and visions is not some clever new revelation that suddenly sprang up in this century. It has been God's idea for thousands of years.

He's the one who gives you the power to envision something that does not yet exist. And since He is a God of intention, His spirit will often prompt you to draft out the vision on paper before taking the first physical step toward its completion.

In Habakkuk 2:2, found in the Old Testament of the Bible, it states: "Write the vision and make it plain on tablets, that he may run who reads it."

Your written vision becomes the strategic road map toward the fulfillment of your dream. And it acts as a compass so you don't lose your way when distraction and opposition come.

Where there is no vision, people perish.
~ Proverbs 29:18, (KJV)

FACT VS. FICTION

Today more than ever before, there is a rising number of people whose dream it is to become a successful actor, model, musician, writer, or athlete. There's nothing wrong with pursuing these professions if it's what God calls you to do.

If He intends for you to take part in this kind of work, then He will equip you with the corresponding gifts and talents to coincide with those desires.

Sadly, an insatiable appetite for fame has distorted reality for some people. Their inability to recognize their true gifts and talents has caused them to pursue a profession that is in no way linked to their natural, God-given abilities.

There are countless gifts and talents of untold worth God has graciously bestowed upon mankind. Unfortunately, some people place no value on those abilities that do not garner praise from the masses or public recognition.

But just because a particular gift or talent doesn't find its way into the celebrity limelight, we shouldn't discard its value and relevance. That would be a huge mistake.

I consider it an absolute travesty to throw away your gifts and talents merely because they are unlikely to bring fame and fortune. When we leave this world, each of us will have to give an account to God of how we used our gifts and talents. In light of that, you should never take for granted what you've been given. Make the most of them!

When it comes to your vision, how can you discern myth from reality, fact from fiction, and truth from a lie? How can you know if what you are entertaining is a godly dream or an earthly delusion? In many instances, the answer lies in exercising common sense.

> *We are always more anxious to be distinguished for a talent which we do not possess than to be praised for the fifteen which we do possess.*
>
> ~ Mark Twain, American author and humorist

Over the years, I have attended many fund-raising events for a variety of worthy causes. On one of those occasions I had the pleasure of meeting basketball giant Shaquille O'Neil, one of the special guests.

The staff photographer for the evening asked Shaq and myself if we would pose for a publicity shot together. Shaq is a big music fan who grew up listening to many of the recording artists I played behind, so we shot the breeze about music while we were preparing to pose for the photo shoot.

Despite the fact that he's bigger than most grizzly bears, the man has a warm and gentle soul so I jokingly asked him, "If basketball didn't work out for you Shaq, would you have considered being a horse jockey?" He lost it and started cracking up.

> *I think knowing what you cannot do is more important than knowing what you can.*
>
> ~ Lucille Ball, American actress and comedienne

I stand six feet tall, but next to Shaq I looked more like one of the Hobbits from The Lord of the Rings movies. Seriously, can you imagine Shaq on a horse at the Kentucky Derby? Now that would be absolutely hilarious, and I'd definitely pay to see it. But let's get real. Any horse carrying Shaq would look like a Shetland pony under duress.

Here's the point I'd like to make. If you're as big as Shaq but imagine yourself winning the Kentucky Derby as a jockey, then you're likely delusional. And that's quite a bit different than dreaming.

Don't get me wrong. I want to encourage you to dream—and dream big! But you can't disregard the common sense God gave you in determining where to direct your efforts.

> *Common sense is the genius of humanity.*
>
> ~ Johann Wolfgang von Goethe, German writer and politician

In today's celebrity-hungry climate, many people discard the truth in exchange for a lie they desperately want to believe. And just because you believe something with all of your heart, it won't make it true unless it actually is true.

If you choose to ignore the indisputable truth in your life, it will eventually result in major disappointments. Our society has entered a day and age when multitudes have traded in priceless truth and valuable common sense for delusional reasoning, which brings about the birth of nightmares rather than dreams.

American Idol and programs of this nature are a great example of how oblivious many have become to the truth. Based on genuine musical gifting, some of the people auditioning have no business doing so.

> *Those who dream by day are cognizant of many things which escape those who dream only by night.*
>
> ~ Edgar Allan Poe, American author and poet

Even an untrained ear can decipher which of those people have no musical talent. The even crazier thing is how stunned those contestants look when they're dismissed. A few of them have even gotten downright angry and belligerent. All of this just goes to show how clueless some people have become to reality.

Such an unwarranted presumption would be like me showing up at the courthouse for a prominent trial with the expectation I'd be handed the position of district attorney even though I have zero aptitude, training, and experience in the field of law. It's absolutely ridiculous to have these kinds of unreasonable and unfounded expectations.

> *The truth that makes men free is for the most part the truth which men prefer not to hear.*
>
> ~ Herbert Agar, American journalist and newspaper editor

Due to a lack of godly vision and genuine purpose, some in our society have developed an unhealthy desire for fame as a means of self-acceptance and approval. I believe this epidemic has caused an entire generation to drink the Kool-Aid of willful ignorance.

In the process, they lose their ability to discern between truth and

> *Death isn't the greatest loss in life. The greatest loss is what dies inside of us while we live.*
>
> ~ Norman Cousins, American political journalist and professor

fiction. When you abandon your God-given ability to discern truth, you will be sentenced to wander the earth aimlessly and potentially miss out on the real dreams God has for you.

DREAM PROOF

Many great visions come to us while we sleep because it's the only time we're disconnected from our sense of skepticism. In that state, God is able to communicate with us on an entirely different plane of consciousness and we are then able to entertain the impossible. Some of our best ideas are given to us as gifts from God as we sleep.

Here's one terrific example. In addition to being a member of the Beatles, Paul McCartney is one of the most prolific and successful songwriters of our time. He noted that the melody to the Beatles' hit song *Yesterday* came to him in a dream back in 1965.

The Guinness Book of World Records lists it as one of the most covered songs in recorded music history, with more than 2,200 cover versions of the song. According to performing rights organization BMI, the song was performed more than 7 million times in the twentieth century. Not a bad dream by any means.

Paul is not the only person who's had a profound dream that materialized into an incredible blessing. Among the most notable is Sarah Breedlove.

Sarah was born in 1867 on a plantation near Delta, Louisiana, where her parents worked as slaves. Sarah is widely credited as being the first female self-made millionaire in America.

Her amazing good fortune stemmed from a scalp disorder that caused Sarah to lose much of her hair. The cure for her hair loss came in the form of a dream.

She is quoted as saying, "One night, I had a dream, and in the dream a big black man appeared to me and told me what to mix up for my hair. I made up my mind I would begin to sell it."

Sarah—who changed her name to Madame C.J. Walker—had been praying for a solution and this is how the answer came. As a result of her divine dream, Sarah founded the Madame C.J. Walker Manufacturing Company, which specialized in hair care for African-American women. The company is still in business today!

Madame C.J. Walker had much higher goals than becoming wealthy. She had strong personal convictions and wanted to make a difference with her life. In fact, she was an early civil rights activist, education advocate, and philanthropist.

From advancements in medicine, science, and the arts to technological innovations that changed the world, God has always spoken to men and women through dreams and will continue to do so. The question is whether you're paying attention to your own dreams and are willing to act upon them.

> *There is no royal flower-strewn path to success. And if there is, I have not found it for if I have accomplished anything in life it is because I have been willing to work hard.*
>
> ~ Madame C.J. Walker

I will praise the Lord, who counsels me;
even at night, my heart instructs me.
~ Psalm 16:7

The wonderful thing about dreams is that it's impossible for you to doubt their content while in the midst of them. In that altered state, you're incapable of talking yourself out of whatever is being communicated—nor can you stop the dream from occurring.

This makes it possible to receive whatever God is trying to download to you, and He's always willing to transmit information for your benefit.

In some instances, He may come to your rescue in the form of a warning of some kind. Who knows how many tragedies and calamities have been avoided because of a dream that helped steer an individual away from danger.

> *The problems of the world cannot possibly be solved by skeptics or cynics whose horizons are limited by the obvious realities. We need men who can dream of things that never were.*
>
> ~ John Keats,
> English poet

Whether it's a song, building, book, solution, design, product, or a cure of some sort, the key to fulfilling those dreams is to wake up, respond in trusting, childlike faith, and act upon what came to you in the dream.

Only the child inside of you has the courage to wage a successful war against the cowardly skeptic who seeks to control you in the hours while you're awake.

VENTURING ONWARD

If you allow Him, God will make use of all the natural gifts and talents He gave you to accomplish His purposes for your life. You should take comfort in knowing that God will never ask you to be someone He didn't intend for you to be.

Neither will He expect you to execute a task of which you're incapable. But this doesn't mean He won't stretch you well beyond your comfort zone and call upon you to do things you feel unqualified to do.

In spite of perceived limitations, He wants you to move forward by faith, and look beyond your current circumstances to Him for the results. As you display the necessary courage to walk into uncharted territory, He will turn an ordinary effort into an extraordinary outcome simply because He's God and He can.

God has Herculean-size dreams He wants you to experience, but an expansive framework that can support the enormous size of the vision must accompany those dreams. This requires working hard, paying close attention to details, and exercising great patience.

Some dreams can take many years to come to fruition. J.R.R. Tolkien's epic trilogy, The Lord of the Rings, took him 12 years to write. Some even suggest it was closer to 17 years from start to finish, including several rewrites and additions.

Despite the enormous investment of time and intense labor, it became the second-bestselling novel ever written, with sales reported to be more than 150 million books since its initial release in 1954.

Apparently, good things do take time. If you want to produce something of real significance in your life, you must take the time to do your best work.

Ultimately, the bigger the dream God gives you, the more resistance you'll feel and the more often you'll be tempted to give up along the way. All the more reason you need to develop a strong sense of patience and resilience, neither of which can be acquired without pressure and opposition.

> *If you have built castles in the air, your work need not be lost; that is where they should be. Now put the foundations under them.*
>
> ~ Henry David Thoreau, American author and philosopher

You will earn your stripes in the trenches of real-life battle. Fulfilling God's dreams will require a heavenly inspired hostility toward everything that tries to prevent it. It's a fight for sure, but it's a battle worth fighting. Much of the outcome hinges on your willingness to engage in the battle and your refusal to concede.

The problem with so many of us, is that we get too anxious for immediate results. This reminds me of the impatient father who tries to assemble his child's Christmas present before reading the step-by-step instructions.

From an unwillingness to follow directions in an orderly fashion, he quickly becomes frustrated, and in his anger, he tosses the toy across the room and aborts the mission—all of this to the bewildered disappointment of his observing child.

> *The most common trait I have found in all successful people is that they have conquered the temptation to give up.*
>
> ~ Peter Lowe, American success strategist and author

Those are the same type of people who give up on their dreams due to a lack of willingness to follow a specific set of instructions. It's really no secret that God's dreams require an arsenal of knowledge before you can begin the assembly process.

God's dreams for you always have order and structure to them, and are only realized by your willingness to work within the framework and follow those orders to the T.

DREAMING ON PURPOSE

If you can accomplish your dream without God's assistance, then trust me, your dream is way too small. All God-inspired dreams require dependency on Him.

But here's the catch. You must work as if everything is dependent upon you, and trust as if everything depends upon Him. Ultimately, it's His direction, timing, and favor that enable your divine dream to come to life.

Otherwise, they're just man-made dreams in which He plays no part. Those can be accomplished merely by utilizing worldly tactics of control, manipulation, bribery, coercion, cheating, lying, stealing, and a host of other ungodly schemes that men use to climb the ladder of external success.

Those kinds of self-indulgent endeavors, however, will lack the profound impact that a genuine dream from God would have. His dream for you is never really just about you anyhow. Nor is it about attaining success for success's sake.

As you read in chapter one, your personal and vocational pursuits will cease to satisfy the deeper longings of your heart and soul if God's presence fails to surround them.

There is a divine purpose attached to the fulfillment of God's dreams for your life. The focus from His perspective is on those who will benefit from what you have to offer as you live out that dream.

Remember, life is comprised of momentary encounters with other people, and your dream will enable you to inspire, touch, and impact as many of them as you can during those connecting points.

In my own life, I would eventually come to understand that the dream God gave me as a young man to write a drum book served a much deeper purpose than I realized.

The release and eventual success of *The Commandments of R&B Drumming* was never really about me. It was about what God wanted to accomplish through me.

As the book circulated around the world and grew in popularity, it became a powerful tool to inspire a multitude of drummers to unlock their own potential. This helped them further develop the gift of rhythm they were given. In the end, my fulfilled dream enabled others to grow and eventually soar musically.

Through the years, I've had the honor of hearing from thousands of people who expressed to me how much my book inspired them and became a tremendous source of joy.

I felt a divine sense of satisfaction knowing I was fulfilling God's dream by taking part in work that was clearly making a difference. I have felt this same divine sense of satisfaction on numerous occasions when I was on the receiving end as well.

During one particular autumn season, I took a group of my drum students from Belmont University in Nashville, Tennessee, to Indianapolis, Indiana, to hear two of the world's greatest drummers perform.

One was a true man of God who has maintained a zeal and love for Jesus. The other was an intellectual who did not have a relationship with God. They both played magnificently.

But there was something that hit my students in a significant way when the man of God played, and it was powerful. It was as if a host of heavenly angels showed up the moment the man walked on stage.

From his first cymbal crash, you could feel an undeniably glorious presence that lit up the room. As he played for the eager listeners, a supernatural joy was released in the venue that literally changed the atmosphere.

> *Christians should never fail to sense the operation of an angelic glory. It forever eclipses the world of demonic powers, as the sun does a candle's light.*
>
> ~ Beverly Sills, American operatic soprano

All of my students picked up on it, and without me saying a thing. They mentioned to me that the drummer who was the man of God (something they were unaware of at the time) had a very profound effect on them.

They acknowledged that the other one was great too, but that his drumming failed to hit them in that deep place in their spirit.

Without being able to verbalize it, they were acknowledging and discerning for themselves the presence of almighty God on a man's drumming and how it touched them. Intellectual ability that lacks the presence of God can dazzle our intellect, but it will fail to stir our heart in that deeply spiritual sense.

God always speaks to people in their hearts, and often enlists other willing individuals to do the speaking for Him as they exercise their gifts and talents. That is what God's presence does to a life that is submitted to Him.

It literally causes people to sense His presence through whatever gift is being shared. This is precisely why you should grant God permission to be in your life and take residency in your heart.

When His presence surrounds you, it's as if heaven is invading earth. And when that happens, everything changes supernaturally. As you go about your daily affairs with God's presence all around you, the lives of others are forever touched.

Suddenly, in the blink of an eye, hope is restored, purpose is reassured, laughter is ignited, and love is rekindled simply because you showed up on the scene and did what you do.

No work done in service to God—making use of your unique gifts and talents—is unimportant because everything you undertake in one way or another affects people.

You are here to touch people on this planet, and fulfilled dreams allow you to touch so many more because they are the means by which God multiplies your capacity to impact.

Let this be a reminder of how important it is for you to fulfill God's dreams for your life. And may this revelation serve as your inspiration for not giving up when the going gets tough.

Remember, the purpose of your dream is to glorify God with a spirit of excellence so others might see, feel, and know Him through the work you accomplish.

> *I can't believe there are many heights that can't be scaled by a man who knows the secret to making dreams come true. This special secret can be summarized in four C's. They are Curiosity, Confidence, Courage and Consistency, and the greatest of these is Confidence. When you believe a thing, believe it all over, implicitly and unquestionably.*
>
> ~ Walt Disney, American entertainment industry icon and theme park creator

DREAM: A QUICK SUMMARY

- Dreams require you to create a corresponding plan of action.
- There is a difference between a godly dream and an earthly delusion; you must learn to discern between the two.
- God will always make use of the gifts and talents He gave you to fulfill the dream.

- All God-size dreams will be met with resistance, so you must choose to persevere.
- God's dreams for you were meant to glorify Him and serve others.
- If you can accomplish your dream without God, your dream was way too small.

Your Personal Prayer

Dear God,
I ask You to awaken the dreams that You have placed deep in my heart and teach me how to dream with You. I invite You to speak to me in every possible way so I might be better acquainted with those dreams that You have for my life. I ask You to forgive me for abandoning any of the dreams You had for me in the past and instill in me the courage necessary to pursue each new one with all I have. I humbly ask for Your divine favor to bring the dream to life so I might please You and be a blessing to Your people. Amen.

4

STRATEGIZE

Formulate a Plan

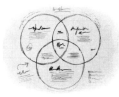

*Being busy does not always mean real work. The object of all work
is production or accomplishment, and to either of these ends
there must be forethought, system, planning, intelligence and honest
purpose, as well as perspiration. Seeming to do is not doing.*

~ Thomas Edison, American inventor and businessman

As you've now learned, my dream of becoming a drummer was ignited by a fourth-grade talent show during which I played on a cardboard box with my hands.

You might be wondering how I went from the elementary school auditorium to playing the biggest, most famous stages of the world. The answer is…I had plan. I always had a plan.

If you want to transform your dreams into successful reality, you too must create a strategy and formulate a plan. Welcome to life principle No. 4 and the undeniable truth that every person who accomplishes something significant does so by way of a plan.

The first step in strategizing and planning involves establishing definitive goals. What has always worked best for me is writing down a goal—and the steps I'll need to take—long before I take action.

Doing this requires time and immense forethought. Let me tell you from experience and from listening to the stories people have shared with me—failing to write down what you want to achieve is like an architect trying to erect a structure without accurate blueprints.

No dream can ever begin to take shape without a plan, and mine was no exception.

When I was 16, I knew it was time to create a plan for my dream. I began to devise a strategic plan for how I would get there. But before I could write out anything on paper, I had to define my objective.

Defining my objective meant I would have to give some serious thought to where exactly I wanted to end up and what specifically I wanted to accomplish as a musician.

After much thought, I decided that my objective was to become an in-demand drummer for world-renowned recording artists. Having that defined objective was really the first step of formulating my plan because everything else was built around that singular vision.

After that, I was ready for the second step, which was to investigate what it would take to get there. Reading magazine interviews and books on musicians who achieved success was how I initially acquired the basic information.

This revelation helped me to further develop my strategy. I discovered the majority of successful drummers I admired developed their musical potential by taking private lessons from the best teachers available. Some even went to music school to get formal training.

To gain more information for my plan, I began asking experienced musicians for their advice on how to go about pursuing my musical dream.

More than once, I was told that if I wanted to increase my chances of success, I would need to move to Los Angeles, because it was the epicenter of the music industry.

At the time, I was a junior in high school and living in Grants Pass, Oregon, a small mountain town that offered no opportunities to fulfill my musical aspirations.

Once armed with this critical insight about the necessity of relocation, I was able to begin setting up some short-range goals. Please keep in mind too that you can't map out short-range goals without at least a basic understanding of the situation or profession you're pursuing.

HOW TO ESTABLISH THE PLAN

A short-range goal is generally something you can accomplish within about a year's time or less. Below is the initial list of short-range goals I established for myself.

Short-Range Goals

- Secure a job in order to finance my musical dreams.
- Take private drum lessons from the best teachers in my area.
- Get in the school band program to learn how to play with an ensemble.
- Begin purchasing classic albums to develop a repertoire of songs.
- Buy a professional set of drums and other necessary musical equipment.
- Play with a professional band to gain essential playing experience.

Topping this list was the most important of my short-range goals: secure some kind of employment. Having a job was the key to reaching my other short-range goals that followed.

Each of those goals was prioritized by order of importance, and each built on the previous one. Remember, you can't climb to the top of a mountain without starting at the bottom.

Fortunately, I managed to secure employment by working two

full-time jobs during the summer. And during the school year, I had an after-school job as well as a weekend one.

Those jobs provided me with the income I needed to make the necessary investments toward my future. With a lot of hard work, I was able to accomplish each of the short-range goals. That gave me a solid foundation on which to build my career.

My short-range goals became my blueprints, and they kept me headed in the right direction even when stuff in life tried to throw me off. Though I couldn't be certain exactly how my plan would unfold, having a solid plan made all the difference in the world.

Next came long-term goals, which are plans based on something you want to accomplish further in the future. They typically won't come together very quickly because they are much more involved than short-term goals.

There is no specified amount of time it takes to achieve long-term goals because they can vary greatly depending on the difficulty of the goal. It could take anywhere from one to 10 years or more depending on the magnitude of the vision. Listed below are the long-range goals I established for myself at the onset of my pursuit.

> *Formulate and stamp indelibly on your mind a mental picture of yourself as succeeding. Hold this picture tenaciously. Never permit it to fade. Your mind will seek to develop the picture.*
>
> ~ Norman Vincent Peale, American minister and author

Long-Range Goals

- Move to Los Angeles after high school graduation to pursue my dream.
- Make contacts and develop strong relationships with other like-minded young musicians.
- Study with a world-renowned drummer who could show me the ropes.

- Land a gig with a major recording artist and tour the world.
- Establish my reputation as a world-class drummer and create a demand for my services.
- Sign endorsement deals with major drum equipment manufacturers.
- Prosper financially through the employment of my gifts and talents.

At the start of my senior year in high school, my family moved to Eugene, Oregon. It proved to be a good move because there were more musical opportunities in Eugene, since it was a college town with a larger population.

Right after my high school graduation, I successfully landed a gig with my first professional working band in Eugene. The band's short-range goal was to travel to Anaheim, California, to score a gig at Disneyland as the house band in the *Tomorrowland Terrace*.

> *If you want to be happy, set a goal that commands your thoughts, liberates your energy and inspires your hopes.*
>
> ~ Andrew Carnegie, American industrialist and philanthropist

Though we did manage to audition for Disneyland, we didn't get the gig. And while the bandleader tried desperately to secure some gigs at local bars, it didn't work out, and the band fell apart.

Despite the failed attempt at Disneyland, I was able to accomplish my first long-range goal—get to Los Angeles where more opportunities existed for those with musical dreams.

At last, here I was, back in my hometown of Los Angeles with my whole future in front of me. It was an exciting time loaded with possibilities.

My sister, Patricia, was living in Beverly Hills and working as a model at the time. She invited me to stay with her for a while to see if I could drum up any gigs in that part of town.

That brought me to my second long-range goal, which was to start making contacts with serious young musicians who shared the same vision of success.

I was 18 and smart enough to realize musicians weren't going to magically appear. I needed a plan. After I did a little research, I decided to take a trip to Beverly Hills High School to try and meet some people who were close to my age.

I showed up at lunchtime on a bright, sunny California day with a plan to attract attention to myself. I brought a pair of drumsticks, a drum practice pad, and a big boom box to crank my music.

I sat on the lawn wearing a very stylish hat, sunglasses, and a chic yellow silk outfit that only a blind man could have missed. I started jamming along with the latest Earth, Wind & Fire album then moved on to some of the current funk hits of the day.

Within a few minutes, I had successfully piqued the curiosity of a few young musicians who couldn't seem to resist coming up to me to find out who I was.

One of those kids was Lenny Kravitz. Lenny and I hit it off right away and became the best of friends. Who would have known that Lenny would go on to become a mega rock star and actor?

Lenny, a handful of other kids I met that day, and I started playing together. They showed faith in my abilities right after our first jam session and began recommending me for various professional gigs in the greater Los Angeles area.

Those referrals led to me establishing a wider network of contacts, which then broadened my work opportunities and enabled me to gain the necessary valuable experience I needed to hone my skills.

My plan definitely worked, and the friendships I formed with a few key individuals that day eventually led to the fulfillment of all my other long-range goals.

> *Imagination is everything. It is the preview of life's coming attractions.*
>
> ~ Albert Einstein, German theoretical physicist

With God's favor, I continued working very hard, pursuing and achieving my long-term goals. I began to soar as I had envisioned, and it felt unbelievably good.

What are you envisioning for yourself? More importantly, what steps are you taking to fulfill that vision? Are you being intentional and strategic with your efforts? Have you mapped out your own plan in any form? Have you prioritized your goals?

The importance of writing out goals and visions can never be overstated. Before hitting it big, Jim Carey was just another struggling actor dreaming of success. In an interview with Oprah Winfrey, Jim shared how he wrote himself a check for $10 million in 1985 when he was broke and things weren't going so well.

He postdated the check 10 years, made it payable to Jim Carey for acting services rendered and kept it in his wallet until it eventually disintegrated. In the same interview, Jim went on to confirm that in 1995 he was paid $10 million for acting services rendered in the movie *Dumb and Dumber*.

> *Our goals can only be reached through the vehicle of a plan, in which we must fervently believe and upon which we must vigorously act. There is no other route to success.*
>
> ~ Pablo Picasso, Spanish painter and sculptor

THINKING THINGS THROUGH

You'll also need to learn how to think things through and develop strategic thinking skills to maximize your full potential.

In my early twenties, I invented a useful product for musicians that I wanted to get on the market. Despite my rather lofty goal, I had no idea how to accomplish this task. A friend suggested I hire a marketing expert who could walk me through the process.

This would be a serious investment, but if I wanted to see my vision come to life I'd have to plunk down some big bucks. Having always been a big dreamer, I was willing to take the risk and decided to go for it.

Each week, I met with the marketing guru and he drilled me with perplexing questions that dumbfounded me. Then he'd send me home to do the necessary research and have me come back the following week with the answers. Initially, I would come back with rather vague answers, and he would respond with, "Humor me with specifics."

The task of uncovering those specifics was enough to make most people run for the hills, and I was tempted to do just that myself. But I decided to meet the challenge and was determined to find the answers no matter how incredibly difficult it might prove to be.

What I eventually learned was that Mr. Marketing Guru was teaching me how to think critically and strategically. I discovered that *thinking* is actually really, really hard work. In fact, it's the hardest work there is.

Few people are willing to put that much thought into their own ideas, visions, and dreams, because it's mentally exhausting work that requires much forethought and agonizing detail.

To think strategically, you must put the necessary time aside because no one thinks clearly when they're in a rush. Many of us have busied our lives with so much activity that we leave ourselves virtually no time to think through things that are of great importance.

Your future is of great importance, and it's imperative that you give it some serious thought. If you don't, your dreams, visions, gifts, and talents might just vaporize.

> *Thinking is the hardest work there is, which is probably the reason so few engage in it.*
>
> ~ Henry Ford, American industrialist and founder of Ford Motor Company

Thinking is like journeying through a maze, in that it will naturally take you down a series of secret passages that lead you on a quest for the solutions you seek.

Finding the answers, however, can be as challenging and confusing as getting to the center of a highly complex labyrinth.

Have you given much thought to your ideas, visions, and dreams? If you haven't, it's doubtful they'll come together. Don't be afraid to think a matter all the way through.

World-renowned neurosurgeon Ben Carson stated, "God has given to every one of us more than fourteen billion cells and connections to our brain."

It is my belief that God intended for us to use this incredibly complex organism. But just like any other muscle in our body, the brain has to be exercised. Thinking is calisthenics for the brain and the means by which God has allowed us to accomplish difficult tasks.

I liken this process of thinking something through to someone who has an idea for a movie, but she must flush that idea out fully. Before she can hope to sell her screenplay, she must develop each scene, one at a time, word by word, until she has a finished script.

Anyone can come up with a basic plot for a movie. But moving past a vague idea for a story to actually developing a full-blown detailed screenplay is an entirely different thing.

After completing my time with my marketing pro, I was able to envision the big picture and take an idea through the many stages of development to completion. I also learned how to analyze and evaluate each segment of a vision, and then put the pieces together in an orderly manner.

In the end, I had developed a prototype for a very useful product and an accompanying well-constructed marketing plan. Unfortunately, I was unable to get it on the market. I considered it a failed attempt

> *Would you like me to give you a formula for success? It's quite simple, really. Double your rate of failure. You are thinking of failure as the enemy of success. But it isn't at all. You can be discouraged by failure or you can learn from it. So go ahead and make mistakes. Make all you can. Because, remember, that's where you will find success.*
>
> ~ Thomas J. Watson Sr., American industrialist and former president of IBM

at reaching for the stars, and a tremendous waste of my hard-earned money. Still, I learned very valuable lessons.

I'm never one to give up simply because an idea doesn't work out. I kept trying out ideas and taking chances. In the process, I was failing forward, onward and toward bigger things that awaited me in the future.

Eventually, the risk I took by investing in that marketing advice would pay off in big ways. The disciplined thinking was responsible for my ability to develop each of my newer goals in stages—a strategy that led to many future successes where I would experience liftoff over and over again. In fact, I am still employing these principles.

This book you're reading is a current example. I've had to think through the entire vision of this book over and over and over again. I have undergone several re-writes and the intense process of tweaking, shaving, sifting, and refining each component of the manuscript to bring a sharp focus to it.

It has taken much deliberate thought to bring this book to a place of excellence that would command your attention and be worthy of your time and money—all with the hope of *Soar!* being able to help you.

Have you ever had a great idea for something you thought could be the catalyst for your own success? I bet you have.

In actuality, most people at one time or another have pondered on great ideas that could propel them toward success. The problem is that so few of them are willing to discipline themselves enough to develop the strategic thinking skills needed to bring that idea to fruition.

There's always a cost for you to acquire those paradigm shifts in your thinking. As the saying goes, if you want to sit in the luxury box seats so many people dream about, then you must be willing to pay the price of admission.

> *I can give you a six-word formula for success: 'Think things through, then follow through.'*
>
> ~ Edward Rickenbacker, American fighter ace in World War I and Medal of Honor recipient

BE INTENTIONAL

No one ever reaches his or her potential for excellence without learning how to think strategically and working past the point of exhaustion.

When I think of someone who was willing to pay the price to reach greatness in order to live up to his potential, I think of martial arts legend Bruce Lee.

Known for his incredible discipline and dedication to his art form, Bruce was a master strategist in every sense of the word. Many people assume all he did was train specifically in the area of martial arts to be the world's greatest.

Untrue. Not only did he engage in rigorous martial arts regimes that few of his competitors would dare attempt, but he also trained intensely in the areas of physical conditioning and nutrition.

Bruce was doing so at a time when none of those things were in vogue. By contemplating on his pursuit of excellence, he perceived what it would take to reach his full potential, developed a cutting-edge strategy that would get him there, and made the extra effort.

How about this bit of additional fascinating information? Bruce was also an accomplished dancer and boxer.

It was the combination of these intricate art forms that formed the basis for his awe-inspiring choreographed fight scenes in his movies. There was incredible intention in everything this man did, and it was all thoroughly planned out in advance.

Bruce may or may not have written his goals out on paper as some do, but he certainly formulated a plan in his heart, mind, and soul and then, step-by-step, he followed that strategic plan. That's how to become a legend, my friend.

In his own words, Bruce once stated, "The key to immortality is first living a life worth remembering."

Perhaps you have a really lofty goal and something you want to be remembered for. As you can see by Bruce Lee's example, it wasn't any one particular skill set that defined him, but rather, it was a combination of all of those incredible disciplines that allowed him to maximize his potential and reach greatness.

As a whole, Bruce was greater than the sum of his parts. You must keep the principle of diversity in mind too as you develop your own gifts and talents, because each new skill you acquire helps to create the total sum of you.

Ever since I was a child, I have had this instinctive urge for expansion and growth. To me, the function and duty of a quality human being is the sincere and honest development of one's potential.

~ Bruce Lee

Few people realize the amount of strategic planning and preparation that go into a high-level performance of any kind. Be it preparation for a fight scene in a movie or an incredible dining experience, preparation is the process that many people forsake, to their own detriment and regret.

Anything of real value takes an incredible amount of time to bring to life. Think about it for a moment.

You can watch an epic movie in three hours that took several years to produce. You can read a biography over a few days that took the author a lifetime to research. You can watch an Olympic event in a couple of minutes that took the athlete a decade to prepare for.

You get the picture. It's considerably easier and quicker to consume something than it is to produce it. But if people didn't produce, what accomplishments, advancements, and enjoyments would be missing from our world?

Diligence in mapping out your vision, patience in preparation, and perseverance in production are the keys to unlocking your full potential and releasing the greatness that lies within you.

History gives us many examples of those who have reached greatness by way of their strategic thinking, planning, and discipline.

For example, Fred Astaire, considered the best dancer of all time by many, created a very detailed plan with regard to the choreography for his movies. He maintained a laser-sharp focus on the intricacies of his dance moves and would not settle for anything less than his personal best.

When it came to preparing for a single dance number in a film, Fred would undertake very physically grueling rehearsals for up to three weeks for a mere 90 seconds of screen time.

With that level of commitment and forethought, it's no wonder he made his dancing look so effortless. Fred's incredibly graceful and rhythmic style was forged out of hours and hours of planning, and that plan provided a way for his gift to shine before millions.

In case you're thinking it was all easy for Fred, check this out. At his first movie screen test, the MGM director stated on paper about Astaire: "Can't act. Can't sing. Slightly bald. Can dance a little."

Fred kept that note at his Beverly Hills mansion all his life as a reminder of how far he had come. Fred used those words as motivation to develop a strategy for success, and it fueled his desire to prove the director wrong.

Fred's enduring work inspired an entire generation of new dancers including the King of Pop, Michael Jackson, who even cited Fred as a major influence. Who would have thought?

How does Fred Astaire connect with your world? He had a dream of becoming

> *Never underestimate the power of dreams and the influence of the human spirit. We are all the same, all the same in this notion. The potential for greatness lives within each of us.*
>
> ~ Wilma Rudolph, American track and field athlete and Olympic champion

> *The search for what you want is like tracking something that doesn't want to be tracked. It takes time to get a dance right, to create something memorable.*
>
> ~ Fred Astaire

a great dancer. After the dream was conceived in his heart, he began to set realistic goals, and then developed a strategy and timeline for how he would reach those goals. You can do the same with the dreams, talents, and gifts God gives you.

Strategizing helps break down a God-size dream into smaller manageable segments, which in turn makes it feel possible to attain.

Your willingness to organize your time in a way that aligns itself with your goals is another key strategy to maximizing your efforts. This keeps you firmly on the path toward God's dreams in the most efficient manner.

When you're convinced the visions you pursue are God's will for your life, you will inevitably come to the conclusion that your primary job is to devise a step-by-step strategic plan to insure the manifestation of that vision.

Then, with that plan in hand, you can confidently begin to pursue what He has called you to do.

Let's take a look at what I call the anatomy of a strategy. This bullet-point list will help you see the big picture so you can prioritize your efforts in an organized fashion with clarity of vision.

Anatomy of a Strategy

- Define your objective by visualizing what you want to accomplish first.
- Investigate what it would take for you to accomplish that goal.
- Set short range-goals that stair-step you toward that vision.
- Set long-range goals that will give you something worthy to strive for.
- Retool, reassess, and recalibrate the plan as the need arises, and adapt it as conditions and your direction change.

Purposefully planning and passionately pursuing your vision is really authentic faith being lived out in real life. It doesn't look very spiritual.

In fact, it won't even feel very spiritual because it's physically intensive and based on action. To take action, you must invoke an act of will over your mind and convince your body to do something it would choose not to do if it were in charge.

Remember, it's not what you say but what you do that determines the level of impact you'll have with your gifts and talents. To say you are going to do something is one thing. To plan it out and actually do it is quite another. Words are cheap, but action always has a cost.

You will never arrive at the destiny God has prepared for you by accident, nor will you stumble upon greatness. You arrive there in stages that are paved with preparation and intention.

> *Before anything else, preparation is the key to success.*
>
> ~ Alexander Graham Bell, Scottish scientist and inventor

ANOTHER SEASON, ANOTHER PLAN

At the time I wanted to get a publishing deal for my first drum instructional method book, *The Commandments of R&B Drumming: A Comprehensive Guide To Soul, Funk & Hip Hop*, I knew nothing about how to write a proposal for a prospective publisher.

The only thing I did know was that I needed to formulate a written plan as I had successfully done with my past endeavors. Here is the strategic four-point plan laid out in chronological order that landed my first book deal.

4-Point Strategic Book Plan

- **Step 1**—Initiate the book writing process, do the necessary research, and then bring the manuscript to completion. (This took 10 years.)
- **Step 2**—Educate myself on the inner workings of the publishing world through exhaustive research and by purchasing every book on the subject I could find. (This took one year.)
- **Step 3**—Seek out a variety of authors and individuals who possess knowledge and expertise in the publishing field for their insight. (This took another year.)
- **Step 4**—Present a formal book proposal with my manuscript to prospective publishers who specialize in publishing these types of instructional books. (This took one more year.)

After conducting many years of research and consistently refining the vision for my book, I finally completed the manuscript. Like any work of excellence, mine evolved over time.

To accomplish Step 2, I took a trip to the place I always go when I want to learn something—the local bookstore. There, I purchased every title on the subject of how to write a nonfiction book proposal. I bought ten books in all and spent a little more than $150. I was so hungry for this information that I devoured each book in rapid succession.

Bit by bit, I downloaded the pertinent information into the hard drive of my mind. After I was done reading all of them, I was no longer clueless. I was now ready to get the most out of Step 3, which was to glean insight from experts in the field of publishing.

Having at least a basic understanding of the publishing industry better prepared me for my valuable time with the experts in the field. Now I could get more specific with my line of questioning.

For Step 3, I made several phone calls and scheduled as many meetings with authors and other respected individuals who had knowledge of the publishing world. I simply asked them to share their insights with me.

After taking in all of this information, I applied and implemented what I learned from the experts and assembled a top-notch proposal for my book. I was ready for Step 4, which was to present my book to potential publishers.

As you learned in the previous chapter, I was successful at signing a publishing deal and my book became a huge success. This opened up many diverse doors of opportunity for me and proved once again that formulating a plan has always been the key to all of my successes.

In all honesty, there hasn't been a single thing I've accomplished in my life that didn't start off as a vision written out on paper. Each goal would eventually birth a corresponding plan of action for its completion.

> *The older I get the more wisdom I find in the ancient rule of taking first things first. A process which often reduces the most complex human problem to manageable proportion.*
>
> ~ Dwight D. Eisenhower, 34th president of the United States

With this in mind, I have three important questions for you:

1. Are you willing to do the hard work of thinking through the process of what you endeavor to do?

2. Are you willing to set forth short- and long-range goals that are in line with your visions and dreams?

3. Are you willing to invest your time, energy, and resources in the pursuit of the essential information that would otherwise keep you from living out the dream?

If you answered these questions with a "yes," then you're in for a great adventure.

Knowledge is all around you, but it's up to you to stir a hunger inwardly for what you seek to accomplish outwardly. Creating a strategy and then formulating a plan to achieve your goal is the secret hidden in plain view.

A key component in my master strategy was to acquire the necessary knowledge that would help me gain a greater understanding of the principles of publishing.

My initial $150 investment in the books I purchased not only taught me how to write a proper nonfiction book proposal, it also taught me various techniques which I've used to write many other business proposals that were not book related.

In many cases, I was able to propose, negotiate, and secure successful business deals for the particular ventures I was pursuing.

Keep in mind, God gives you visions and dreams that He truly wants you to accomplish. But desire is something He demands you cultivate from within. The proof of your desire lies in whether your passion has consumed you enough to actually devise a winning strategy to get there.

Nothing substantial is ever achieved by coincidence, accident, or happenstance. God's dream for your life will only be realized by formulating a strategic plan and then by following His direction on how to interpret, adjust, and implement that plan. This gives wings to your vision and the eventual birth of those dreams.

Don't measure yourself by what you have accomplished, but by what you should have accomplished with your ability.

~ John Wooden, American basketball player and coach

I have to be honest; fulfilling God's amazing dreams for your life will cost you absolutely everything. If you're not willing to pay the price, you will never reach your potential and be all He created you to be. Nor will you accomplish all He prepared for you to do.

STRATEGIZE: A QUICK SUMMARY

- Achieving greatness, attaining success, and reaching your full potential is never accomplished without a strategy—a plan, system, or methodology of some kind.
- Formulating a plan takes discipline and foresight.
- Developing a strategy is the process of devising a blueprint for what you hope to achieve.
- Planning and strategizing help break down a God-size dream into smaller manageable segments.
- A well-defined strategy helps you combat the opposing forces that challenge your dream.
- Creating a winning strategy requires you to think through the entire process.
- Not having a plan is the biggest reason people fail to make use of God's gifts.

Your Personal Prayer

Dear God,
I ask You to unfold Your divine plan for my life and give me the strategy to prosper in all You call me to do and be. I pray against fear, apathy, laziness, and indifference. I ask You for fresh downloads of wisdom, revelation, and guidance, and a discerning spirit that will enable me to accomplish every task You lay out before me with total confidence that with You all things are possible. Amen.

5

PURSUE

Take Initiative to Reach Your Dreams

*There are many things that will catch my eye, but there are only
a few that catch my heart. ... It is those I consider to pursue.*
~ Tim Redmond, American author and motivational speaker

My dream of becoming a writer goes all the way back to my childhood. I was twelve years old when I suddenly developed a strong desire to write a book on camping.

Eager to get going, I decided to check out every book on the subject from the public library. I began to compile the information I gathered—with the goal of writing a book that was better than all of them.

Needless to say, I had no idea what the word plagiarism meant. Even if I did, I certainly wasn't going to let some weird word stop me from writing my book. After all, I was kid on a mission from God.

The most hilarious part of this story is that I had never been camping. I guess my thinking was that I wanted to camp so badly that I was willing to write about it even if I couldn't do it.

Through my book, I could fantasize about being a mountain man. It's in the heart of every boy to pursue wild, untamed adventure, and I was no different than any other boy.

With the dream of adventure always before me, I worked on my book in the back seat of the car while mom drove around doing errands. The writing continued at the supermarket, the barbershop, the post office, and even in the foyer of my dentist's office. I didn't want to waste a single minute, so I turned each of those visits into a venue for progress.

In retrospect, I can see how God planted the seed in me to write. There would be a great purpose in writing that would be made known to me at a much later time in life.

Despite all the work I put into my book on camping, no publisher was willing to take a chance on me. Nevertheless, I did eventually get to go camping.

And through that initial adventure with writing, God was molding me like clay and preparing in me the heart of a writer. Many years later, I would pursue and gain the opportunity to write my first published article in a leading magazine about my experiences as a musician.

From that time, I began to write, write, write, and was fortunate enough to get published on a regular basis. Still, I had no idea where all of this was headed.

You might say I felt compelled to write for no other reason than I had this un-quenchable desire to inspire people with the power of words. I found writing to be one of the most effective ways to reach people all around the world—so I kept pursuing it.

I never turned down an opportunity to write something that could inspire people, even if I didn't get paid. I felt no door was too small or too big to enter, and no assignment was beneath or above me. I was hungry and willing to put forth my best effort.

> *Great things are not done by impulse, but by a series of small things brought together.*
>
> ~ Vincent Van Gogh, Dutch Post-Impressionist painter

I began developing the necessary skills to enhance my writing gift. And God faithfully opened more opportunities for me to impact the lives of others through that writing platform. I sensed the Lord was with me through all of them and led me to each divine assignment with courage, clarity, and confidence in the pursuit.

His God instructs him and teaches him the right way.
~ Isaiah 28:26

> *Four steps to achievement: plan purposefully, prepare prayerfully, proceed positively, pursue persistently.*
>
> ~ William A. Ward, American author and inspirational writer

This courage for pursuit I speak of came from God's frequent whispers into my spirit. It's as if He was on the sidelines of my life, blowing the warm and gentle winds of confidence over me.

God beckoned me down the path with heavenly assurance. So, I remained faithful to the call and stayed the course. In the past, I had followed this same pattern with regard to my career as a drummer; the results always astounded me.

PRINCIPLES OF PURSUIT

The real power to see your dreams come to fruition is in the doing and pursuing. Once you have formulated a plan, set realistic goals, and strategized how you intend to get there, then comes the real work.

It is through intense labor and by enduring the fiery furnace of frustration that dreams become forged into realities. To pursue is life principle No. 5.

There are three essentials that prove whether your pursuit of something is genuine. They are:

- ➤ desire
- ➤ determination
- ➤ diligence

Anything you accomplish will always begin with earnest desire. If desire is the vehicle that transports you to your destination, then courage is the fuel for that vehicle.

Therefore, you must make sure you pull into the heavenly fuel station of the Lord frequently to fill up the tank. The more you hang out in God's presence, the more courage and confidence will be poured out upon your heart.

When desire simmers long enough, it will give birth to determination—the action component of your equation.

Finally, you must consistently apply diligence to all things if you want to ensure your success. It's important to remember too that while determination can be thought of as ambition applied in a temporary manner, diligence is a long-term discipline.

Anyone can be determined just long enough to achieve a particular goal, only to revert back to complacency when the mission is accomplished. Can you think of a time or two when that happened in your life? It's definitely a common challenge for all of us.

> *Desire is the starting point of all achievement, not a hope, not a wish but a keen pulsating desire which transcends everything*
>
> ~ Napoleon Hill, American author

Diligence is a behavioral characteristic that becomes a way of living. It's a mindset that exhorts, "I will stay committed to my visions and dreams by giving my absolute best work to all that is required of me throughout every phase of my life."

Diligence is best exemplified in the life of inventor Thomas Edison. His relentless dedication led to the invention of the phonograph, motion-picture camera, and the long-lasting, practical, electric light bulb. It's hard to think of a world without this man's contributions. His passionate pursuits improved the quality of life and amplified creative possibilities for all mankind. He literally changed the face of this earth in the process.

In examining the life of someone such as Thomas Edison, most of us would mistake genius for hard work. We tend to think of great achievers as being innately more gifted than ourselves, when in reality they simply worked harder and displayed more courage.

At face value they may seem more gifted, but upon closer investigation you'll discover an intense pursuit that was more laborious than you dared imagine.

But, hey, it's easier to believe those individuals possess more genius than regular people. Thinking that way releases people from the responsibility of having to fully develop and pursue what they've been given.

By taking the easy way out, you can justify your lack of desire to labor intently. Unfortunately, by choosing to believe a lie you leave so much of your untapped potential on the drawing board. And that's really a shame.

> *You gain strength, courage and confidence by every experience in which you really stop to look fear in the face. … you must do the thing you think you cannot do.*
>
> ~ Eleanor Roosevelt, 32nd first lady of the United States

How much more could you impact the world with your gifts and talents if you were willing to work past pain, fear, failure, disappointment and rejection? How much more could you change the landscape of earth if you showed more courage?

In response to his repeated failures, the great Thomas Edison said, "I have not failed; I've just found 10,000 ways that won't work."

Honestly now, how many of us would have kept pursuing a dream, working past our tenth failure, let alone ten thousand? If Edison had stopped trying any earlier than he did, he would have missed his beacon of light and we might all still be in the dark.

He offered more insight by saying, "When you have exhausted all possibilities, remember this—you haven't."

How's that for pursuing and persevering! Statements like that stir me deeply. They prompt me to stop wallowing in self-pity after only a few unsuccessful attempts toward a goal.

Can you relate? Have you ever had a great idea, pursued it, and then gave up because the going got too tough? You must get over yourself and get back into your laboratory and work, work, work. If you do, you can believe that everything will change.

Diligence is a necessary part of God's plan for you to develop and pursue what He gave you. If you apply it, guaranteed, you will see immense growth in the area of your natural giftings and talents.

> *I never did anything by accident, nor did any of my inventions come by accident; they came by work.*
>
> ~ Thomas Edison

Who knows what miraculous things can come about as a result? This is a divine principle that cannot be altered, and anyone who seeks to reach his or her potential must abide by this truth.

EXCELLING AT EXCELLENCE

At this point, you might be asking yourself why in the world you should work so hard and pursue excellence in your life. What's the point of all of this?

First of all, God prewired you with the potential to become excellent within the unique area of your calling—what He wants you to do with your gifts and talents.

Attaining excellence shows God your gratitude for the potential with which He has blessed you. Plus, if you're not working hard in the pursuit of something, you become stagnant and bored. Life becomes uneventful at best.

The opportunity to work hard is actually a divine gift God gave you to make life interesting and meaningful. Having something worthwhile to strive for gives you a reason to wake up each day.

Life really only makes sense when there is something challenging to pursue, something that will demand your best effort, and something that will impact the lives of others.

Here comes the "but" part of my message to you. But, there is a dance that must take place between you and God to enable you to succeed. It's a very intricately choreographed dance where you allow Him to lead.

There are times when God will urge you to move, work, go, push, fight, and stand your ground. There also will be times when you must rest your feet on His feet and let God carry you through the dance.

When my daughter was a little girl, we danced a lot together. And when she got tired or couldn't figure out the steps, I would tell her to place her feet on top of mine and I would dance for her until she was ready again.

It is the same with God. There are times when I've had to learn to not try so hard. Those were the times God was going to do the dancing for me. And I had to be patient and trusting, learning to remain still and allowing God to be God.

The key to being an elegant dancer in tandem with God is simply to put your trust in Him. As that relationship strengthens, you will eventually develop a sixth sense for how He is orchestrating the dance. You will know in your heart when He says rest and wait on Me, or when He says charge ahead.

If you're bored with life—you don't get up every morning with a burning desire to do things—you don't have enough goals.

~ Lou Holtz, American football coach and author

As I shared with you in an earlier chapter, you must learn to work as if everything hinges on your effort and at the same time learn to trust in God as if everything depends upon Him. It's a paradox for sure, but then again, so are many aspects of life.

IN PURSUIT OF A DREAM

American neurosurgeon Ben Carson is a man who personifies the meaning of hard work and understands what it takes to pursue a godly vision to completion.

Ben was the first surgeon in the world to successfully separate Siamese twins. In 1987, he and a 69-member surgical team from Johns Hopkins Hospital in Baltimore, Maryland, worked for 22 hours nonstop to separate the twins who had been joined at the back of the head. It was an astonishing accomplishment.

A lifetime of study, observation, and practice prepared Ben for that pivotal moment in history. Everything he knew and all the experience he had amassed were called upon that day, and it all paid off in a massively jubilant way.

The gifted surgeon understood that developing the potential within himself could change the lives of others forever. This godly motivation fueled his intense drive and gave him the courage to overcome every obstacle that would try and stand in his way.

And there were many challenges Ben faced, going all the way back to his early childhood. You can read about this incredibly purposeful man and his amazing accomplishments in his book, *Gifted Hands: The Ben Carson Story.*

God gives you the honor and privilege of making valuable contributions to the world around you by providing you with the means to utilize your natural talents. Through this labor-intensive process, you're given the opportunity to help your fellow man by improving their lives in some way.

> *I became acutely aware of an unusual ability—a divine gift, I believe—of extraordinary eye and hand coordination. It's my belief that God gives us all gifts, special abilities that we have the privilege of developing to help us serve Him and humanity.*
>
> ~ Ben Carson

Making a difference in the lives of others in a way that only you can, should be the motive and main thrust behind all you do. It was precisely this kind of motivation that inspired Thomas Edison to do his best work. He once reflected, "I never perfected an invention without thinking in terms of how it would benefit others."

Throughout the seasons in your journey of life, certain aspects of your gifting will naturally move to the forefront. At these appointed times, it's important that you begin pursuing and developing those newer skills, as they will help broaden the base of your calling and enhance your overall effectiveness.

Developing each of your talents can be compared to investing in a diversified stock market portfolio. At times, one stock may be more valuable than another. But over time, the goal of the investor is to increase the net worth of his or her entire stock portfolio. Your goal should be the same with regard to your talents.

> *Far and away the best prize that life offers is the chance to work hard at work worth doing.*
>
> ~ Theodore Roosevelt, 26th president of the United States

My primary gift is being a communicator. As a young man, I worked diligently to communicate effectively as a drummer. The focus later included developing my writing skills, paving the way for me to become an author and thus increasing my platform and sphere of influence.

From there, I refined my verbal skills and pursued the motivational speaking work I felt called to. Eventually, this culminated in becoming an educator and mentor. All of my pursuits are related to my primary gift of communication.

You must understand that carefully wrapped up within your preeminent gift are many subsequent gifts that work in direct relation to one another.

Your goal should be to make use of all God has graciously given to you with a spirit of excellence and to reach your full potential in each specific area.

COST OF GREATNESS

> *Every calling is great when greatly pursued.*
>
> ~ Oliver Wendell Holmes Sr., American physician and author

Quincy Jones is one of the "greats" of the music industry. I first met the legendary producer back in 1989 when I was playing at the Soul Train Awards with R&B superstar Bobby Brown.

We became friends, and I remember being intrigued not only by his success but also by Quincy's pursuit of excellence in all he does. If his name isn't familiar to you, I'll bet you recognize his work.

Quincy produced Michael Jackson's *Thriller* album—the biggest selling album of all time. He also worked with such music icons as Ray Charles, Stevie Wonder, and one of my all-time favorites—Frank Sinatra.

One evening, while having dinner with Quincy in New York, I asked him to share some insight on what made Frank such an extraordinary performer and another of the "greats."

Quincy told me that Frank was one of the most highly educated and skilled musicians he has ever known and that he had a work ethic second to none.

Quincy shared a story about the two of them being on a flight together and watching Frank furiously write song lyrics on a pad of paper—over and over and over again.

Frank wrote down the words to the song not only to memorize them for his upcoming live show, but because he wanted them so seared into his consciousness that the song became a part of him.

If you've ever seen Frank Sinatra perform or checked him out on YouTube, you'll now better understand how he sang every song with heart and the deepest conviction. Frank's passionate pursuit of excellence and his willingness to go the extra mile enabled him to maximize his potential and reach greatness.

After that story, I finally understood why watching Frank Sinatra

> *When love and skill work together, expect a masterpiece.*
>
> ~ John Ruskin, English author and social commentator

perform live in concert as a young boy left such an indelible mark on my spirit. Excellence has a way of doing that.

One of the best methods for increasing your capabilities in any given area is to begin compiling a treasure chest of knowledge on the subject that has captivated your heart.

You do this by choosing to become a voracious reader—not spending countless hours surfing the Internet, sharing nonsense on social media, playing video games, or watching mindless reality television shows that steal away your precious time.

Besides immersing yourself in the pursuit of your passion through diligent investigation, you'll need to become an apprentice of a master who is accomplished in the area of your gifts and talents.

> *If people knew how hard I worked to get my mastery, it wouldn't seem so wonderful at all.*
>
> ~ Michelangelo, Italian artist and architect

During the Renaissance period, great artists such as Leonardo da Vinci and Michelangelo didn't ascend to the top of the art world out of the clear blue sky.

There was an essential process they were engaged in that allowed them to fully realize their potential. They studied for many years under the great artisans of their day and accepted the position of apprentice without hesitation.

It was the same with brilliant composers such as Ludwig Van Beethoven and Wolfgang Amadeus Mozart. Each of them had musical mentors who were the most acclaimed teachers in their region.

That is how anyone achieved excellence with regard to their particular gifting in those days. Not surprisingly, the process remains the same for us today.

DO YOU HAVE WHAT IT TAKES?

Unfortunately, many people want to achieve greatness and attain success without making the necessary investment of time and effort. We are rapidly becoming a society that wants something for nothing. And to add insult to injury, we want it now.

Guess what? It doesn't work that way. Forget what you've been told and the lies you've been sold.

Don't only practice your art, but force your way into its secrets; art deserves that, for it and knowledge can raise man to the Divine.

~ Ludwig Van Beethoven, German composer and pianist

You can't possibly become accomplished and develop your full potential by adopting the mind-set of those who feel entitled to success without having to work for it.

That's like expecting to fly first class without paying the extra cost of the airfare, or hoping to look lean and muscular while eating a steady diet of junk food and avoiding exercise.

Some people have the uncanny tendency to imagine themselves on stage but never in the practice room.

To achieve the brilliance of which you're more than capable, you must separate yourself from this current cultural mind-set.

In life, you'll often have to travel with the rest of the crowd. Be that as it may, it's imperative that you get off at a different stop than everyone else if the destination you desire is to be different.

You have no right to anything you have not pursued, for the proof of desire is in the pursuit.

~ Mike Murdock, American televangelist and pastor

If you follow the masses, you'll never be all you can be because, sadly, many people set very low standards and demand very little of themselves. Too many lack vision and are stricken with lethal doses of laziness, apathy, and complacency.

For the most part, the average person chooses to embark upon the path of least resistance and the results they get are, well, average. If being excellent is easy, then everyone would be excellent. Let's not fool ourselves. We know all too well that true excellence demands a superior effort.

> *Following the path of least resistance is what makes men and rivers crooked.*
>
> ~ Larry Bielat, American football coach and author

For example, if you're on a diet to lose a certain amount of weight, its fairly easy in the beginning to lose weight quickly. All you have to do is follow the plan laid out for you. But getting rid of that last bit of surplus when you've already lost a significant amount of weight is much more difficult.

It requires more scrutiny of every detail of your diet and exercise regimen. In reality, it's always more difficult to go from good to great than it is to go from average to good. That's because the gains on the upper spectrum are so much smaller and much more difficult to acquire, because they demand a higher level of discipline.

> *Success, real success, in any endeavor demands more from an individual than most people are willing to offer— not more than they are capable of offering.*
>
> ~ James Roche, American statistician and former CEO of General Motors

Like shaving off that last 1/100 of a second from your best time on the 100-meter dash. Do I shave the hair off my head, back and arms? Should I drink water that's pre-loaded with more electrolytes? There are so many pertinent questions that need to be answered correctly and so much hard work to do to reach that higher ground.

Nevertheless, finding the answers will always come at a higher price and require a much more intensified degree of study on the subject. This ramped-up effort is something few people are willing to entertain because it's so all-consuming.

As an exercise in mental preparation for a future victory, Seattle Seahawks quarterback Russell Wilson attended Super Bowl XLVII to observe and study everything that goes on in the pregame warm-up and on the field in the actual setting of the game. For most NFL players, watching it on television would suffice.

Not so with Russell. He wanted to see how the San Francisco 49ers and Baltimore Ravens handled the pressure up close. He wanted to taste it, feel it, smell it, and analyze the rhythm of the game in person. Russell felt this insight and experience would give him an edge if the time ever came when his team made it there.

Russell set his sights on taking his teammates to the Super Bowl the following year. This was quite an ambitious goal for a young quarterback who'd only been in the NFL for one year.

Amazingly, just one year later as he had envisioned, Russell led the Seahawks to victory in Super Bowl XLVIII by destroying the highly favored Denver Broncos with an unbelievable score of 43 to 8. Another David and Goliath story for sure, and further proof of what choosing to go the extra mile can accomplish.

No matter how hard we work, the truth is that no one has 24 hours a day to hone his or her craft. If it required 24 hours a day to be a master of something, then no one would ever be able to do it.

Fortunately, it's brief periods of intense and radical focus on a frequent and consistent basis that unleash your greatest growth potential.

If you remember this fact, you'll be less likely to waste smaller segments of time. Life is short, so pursue your passion with everything you've got, and be intentional in all you do.

> *No one ever attains very eminent success by simply doing what is required of him; it is the amount of excellence of what is over and above the required that determines greatness of ultimate distinction.*
>
> ~ Charles Kendall Adams, American educator and historian

Today will never happen again. And by tomorrow, today will be gone forever. Remember, it's not the length of one's life that matters most but the intensity with which one has lived pursuing God's vision for his or her life.

God has given each of you a gift from his great variety of spiritual gifts. Use them well to serve one another. Do you have the gift of speaking? Then speak as though God himself were speaking through you. Do you have the gift of helping others? Do it with all the strength and energy that God supplies. Then everything you do will bring glory to God through Jesus Christ. All glory and power to him forever and ever! Amen.
~ 1 Peter 4:10-11 (NLT)

PASSION OF PURSUIT

Through the years, I've received numerous inquiries from drummers all around the world who are interested in studying with me. But none have stood out quite like Daniel Wheeler.

At the top of my initial phone conversation with Daniel, I asked him where he was from.

He replied, "Washington D.C., sir."

My immediate response was, "Do you know I live in Los Angeles?"

Daniel said, "Yes, sir, I do."

I could tell right away Daniel was a teenager so I asked, "Are you planning to come out here with your parents for a family vacation or trip to Disneyland?"

"No, sir," Daniel said. "I would be coming out there specifically to study with you, and for eight hours if that's possible."

My first thought was his parents have a lot of money and were perhaps making an investment in their son's future by affording him this opportunity to fly out to L.A. and gain knowledge from me.

Even if that was the case, I didn't think it was necessary for Daniel to come all the way to California to study with me since there were plenty of good drum instructors on the East Coast.

At that point, I tried to talk him out of it and suggested he study with some first-rate local teachers in the D.C area since this was clearly more convenient.

With a very stern young man's voice he replied, "No, sir, I want to study with you, Zoro. I've seen you in concert a few times and I've also attended a couple of your drum clinics when you were in the D.C. area. After seeing you the first time, I made it my number one goal to study with you. It's my dream, sir."

I went ahead and gave Daniel the dates I was able to work with him. I honestly never expected to hear back from the kid. It wouldn't have been the first time someone scheduled lessons then forgot about it.

What transpired next had the most profound effect on me. Daniel called about an hour before our scheduled lesson time and asked for directions to my house.

When I asked how he traveled to L.A., Daniel told me he took the Greyhound bus—a week's ride across the country—because it was all he could afford. He then told me he bought a second-hand bicycle after getting off the bus so he could ride to my house from the motel where he was staying.

I was blown away! I couldn't believe what I heard. I was fascinated with Daniel's determination, to say the least. I could tell there was something really special about this young man.

When I said goodbye to Daniel after the conclusion of our time together, the last thing I told him was, "Hey, Daniel, one of these days I am going to write a book and tell people the story of your amazing determination. And trust me, son, your story is going to inspire people all around the world."

I have now fulfilled my promise to Daniel.

A few years after my encounter with Daniel, I was giving a drum clinic in the D.C. area, and whom do I see in the audience? You guessed it. Daniel Wheeler. I couldn't resist telling his amazing story to the crowd.

When I finished, the entire audience stood to their feet, cheering and screaming for Daniel. It was a touching moment for both of us and one I will never forget as long as I live.

I have retold this story many times at speaking events, and not surprisingly, it usually floors everyone in attendance. When I think of determination and desire, I think of Daniel Wheeler, who embodied both of these attributes so courageously.

Now, I have three questions for you:

1. Are you pursuing your ambitions with this kind of passion?

2. Are you taking these kinds of risks?

3. Are you exemplifying this kind of courage and determination?

Desire is the key to motivation, but it's the determination and commitment to unrelenting pursuit of your goal—a commitment to excellence—that will enable you to attain the success you seek.

~ Mario Andretti, Italian American race car driving champion

If not, it's likely you will not develop your full potential. This kind of risk, courage, and determination is common among people who succeed at fulfilling God's dream for their life. Now, you must determine in your heart if you are going to be that kind of person.

PURSUE: A QUICK SUMMARY

- Life only makes sense when you have something challenging to pursue.
- Desire, determination, and diligence prove whether your pursuit is genuine.
- Intense labor is a necessary part of God's plan for you to develop what He gave you.
- Attaining excellence in what you were created to do shows God your gratitude for your gifts.
- Short periods of intense and radical focus will produce the most optimum results so you can reach your highest potential.

Your Personal Prayer

Dear God,
I pray that You would ignite a fire and passion inside me so I might labor hard after the things that matter to You. Forgive me for the times I may not have risen up and given life all I am capable of giving. I ask that You would give me a revelation of how much my gifts, talents, and skills can impact the lives of others so I might be diligent to develop them with a true spirit of excellence, in a way that would bring glory and honor to Your name. Amen.

6

BELIEVE

Live by Faith

*Faith is to believe what you do not yet see; the reward
for this faith is to see what you believe.*

~ St. Augustine, Christian theologian and philosopher

At the beginning of December each year, I think about what I want to accomplish in the coming year. Once I have given this serious thought, I begin to draft out goals.

One of my top goals for more than a decade was to write and publish a motivational book that would encourage, equip, and empower musicians and creative people with the tools needed to fulfill their artistic dreams.

Yet despite this being on the top of my list of goals, other demands pushed their way to the forefront. Year after year, the goal was not accomplished.

I had been writing the book during those ten years. Eventually, I completed the manuscript and a full proposal—ready to present to publishers. Unfortunately, every publisher I submitted my book to turned it down.

The good news was that no one turned it down because they thought it wasn't a good book. At the time I was trying to persuade publishers to get my book to market, the United States was mired in the Great Recession. Publishers were buying few book manuscripts and taking even fewer chances on new authors.

I hit a tall, long, thick brick wall; it was a very disappointing time. I began to doubt my timing and wondered how I could have come this close yet still be unable to hit a home run. Frustrated, I asked God, "Lord, how do You expect me to fulfill the vision You gave me of impacting the world through my motivational books if no one wants to publish them?"

I left the manuscript in God's hands and went on to other projects and goals. But in my heart, I never fully gave up believing that the book would someday come to life in God's appointed time.

Have you ever had an experience like that? You believe God has led you a certain direction, but the goal of that direction isn't being fulfilled. What do you do then?

GOD'S DIVINE TIMING

A few more years went by. Then one day I had a sudden urge to revisit the idea of pitching the book. After reading the manuscript again, I realized I needed to revise the entire book.

I spent the next eighteen months writing essentially a new book. I retitled it *The Big Gig: Big-Picture Thinking for Success*. Even though this newer rendition had all of the original core concepts, principles, and elements of the first manuscript, my newer writing style reflected the present-day me.

While in Los Angeles on a business trip in 2008, I met with Alfred Publishing executives and shared my concept for *The Big Gig*. Alfred Publishing is one of the world's largest music instructional method book and sheet music publishers.

The folks at Alfred embraced the book manuscript immediately and truly believed in its potential. They encouraged me to write the book exactly as I envisioned it, and even suggested I retain all of the spiritual insights I had included.

The spiritual freedom I was granted to share my faith was unprecedented. I couldn't have asked for more.

God is so faithful, and sometimes I bow my head in humility at His awesomeness. God led me to the folks at Alfred Publishing, which proved to be the perfect publishing venue for my book.

Through the long and exhaustive publishing process, I discovered that God has divine timing and I had no business trying to rush things.

As excited as I was to see my goal come to fruition, I am extremely grateful God didn't allow it to happen until just the right time. If I had my way, the book would have been out in the marketplace more than a decade earlier. But if published then, the book would not have been anything close to the final version. I grew tremendously as a creative artist and writer during that period. I grew as a husband, father, businessman, and man of God.

With more experience came varied ways of being able to convey a story, a message, a metaphor, and an analogy. I had so many more deep life experiences and amazing stories to share. They gave my writing a depth of character that could not have come any other way.

Since the release of *The Big Gig* in late 2011, I have received countless messages of gratitude from readers of just about every age living in just about every country of the world. Rarely does a day go by when I don't receive some kind of testimony from people who have been encouraged by reading *The Big Gig*.

And to think how close I came to giving up on this dream because of all the rejection I initially faced. When I look back, I am reminded that every day brought with it ample opportunity for discouragement and disappointment.

Yet the only thing that helped me weather all of the storms of self-doubt and disappointment was my childlike faith. I simply refused to stop believing that God could make a way for me to accomplish this dream He placed in my heart.

By placing my trust in God, His grace enabled me to keep believing in Him more than in circumstances. Doing so ultimately paved the way for my success.

> *Our greatest weakness lies in giving up. The most certain way to succeed is always to try one more time.*
>
> ~ Thomas Edison, American inventor and businessman

THE GREATEST GIFT

The act of believing is a human capability that remains among the most miraculous, mysterious, and mystifying forces on earth. Believing is life principle No. 6.

To eliminate our ability to believe is to nullify what makes us uniquely human. Believing is the impetus behind every notable and admirable accomplishment in the history of mankind.

Nothing of significance in your personal, spiritual, and vocational life can be achieved without believing and exercising faith. Your believing serves as the invisible mortar upon which you assemble every thought, idea, conviction, and dream.

More importantly, nothing you do can please God without faith and belief operating simultaneously. They are one in the same and the prerequisite for you to establish a relationship with Him. To do this, you must learn to live from your heart. This is not a matter of intellect. Faith and belief are recognized within your spirit. Believing wholeheartedly requires you to connect with two other human attributes: hope and imagination.

Maybe it will help to remember it this way: Faith, hope, and imagination are as inseparable as cheese, dough, and tomato sauce in a pizza recipe. Each of those essential ingredients serves a different function, yet collectively they are what make the original pizza recipe what it is.

To believe with all your heart, you must latch onto the invisible but clearly discernable substance known as faith. Then you fuse faith with

> *Faith consists in believing when it is beyond the power of reason to believe.*
>
> ~ Voltaire, French writer and philosopher

the unlimited power of your imagination. Combine those two with hope and suddenly incredible possibilities begin to open up in your heart as God intended.

God created you with an extraordinary capacity to believe in the impossible, and He gave you faith as the means to accomplish those impossible tasks.

DON'T STOP BELIEVING!

Louis Zamperini could have never survived 47 days in an inflatable life raft at sea if he didn't believe he could survive.

A former track star who competed in the 1936 Berlin Olympics, Louis's athletic dreams were put on hold when he joined the U.S. Air Corps as a bombardier in the South Pacific during World War II.

On a routine reconnaissance mission, Louis's aircraft crashed into the Pacific Ocean. Thus began his unbelievable battle for survival. During those 47 days, he and another surviving crew member fought off everything from thirst and starvation to shark attacks and violent storms.

Drifting some 2,000 miles into Japanese-controlled waters, Louis was captured while barely alive by the Japanese and held in a prison camp known as Execution Island for nearly three years.

It was a horrific place where every known prisoner up to that point had been put to death. There, he was physically tortured and mentally tormented.

Without the hope of one day being set free, Louis simply wouldn't have survived the brutal physical, mental, and emotional distress he underwent.

It was his belief that a better day was on the horizon that enabled him to endure those hardships. Louis's belief was anchored in his hope.

Amazingly, he lived to tell his absolutely heroic and riveting tale. You can read about Louis in *Unbroken: A World War II Story of Survival, Resilience and Redemption.*

Throughout my own trials, I've been unwilling to discard my God-given power to believe. The older I get, the more I refuse to give up that indomitable childlike faith and believability that have been responsible for so many of the miraculous occurrences in my life.

No matter how much I'm tempted to get jaded by life, I realize I've been given a say in the matter through my free will. If faith is the only gift I can give back to God while I inhabit this earth, then I will choose to go on believing with the heart of a child that all things are possible for him who believes.

And I will unapologetically put my hope and trust in the invisible but certainly knowable God. It's my prayer you will do the same!

And without faith, it is impossible to please God, because anyone
who comes to him must believe that he exists
and that he rewards those who earnestly seek him.
~ Hebrews 11:6

THE POWER OF IMAGINATION

Imagination is part of belief, one of the extraordinary gifts God has given you to impact this world. He gave it to you so you might dream up impossible things that never were and then take the necessary action to make them real.

Albert Einstein once said, "When I examine myself and my methods of thought, I come to the conclusion that the gift of fantasy has meant more to me than my talent for absorbing positive knowledge."

The world's most famous physicist called his imagination a "holy curiosity."

By following your own sense of holy curiosity, you will venture on an extraordinary discovery. As you begin to take practical steps to develop your own limitless imagination, you will find that it will continue to expand to new dimensions.

God wired you to take on the impossible and gave you the power of your imagination and the capacity to believe as the method for accomplishing it. American philosopher Eric Hoffer stated it perfectly when he said, "Man is the only creature that strives to surpass himself and yearns for the impossible."

If you are to accomplish the impossible as God intends, then you must change the way you think so you can see possibilities you have not previously seen.

Here are five powerful quotes to get you thinking beyond what's possible and past your current self-imposed limitations:

1. *We are all faced with a series of great opportunities brilliantly disguised as impossible situations.* (Charles R. Swindoll, American Christian pastor and author)

2. *We would accomplish many more things if we did not think of them as impossible.* (Vince Lombardi, American football player and coach)

3. *Believe and act as if it were impossible to fail.* (Charles F. Kettering, American inventor and businessman)

4. *It always seems impossible till it's done.* (Nelson Mandela, African antiapartheid revolutionary and former president of South Africa)

5. *Without faith nothing is possible. With it, nothing is impossible.* (Mary McLeod Bethune, American educator and civil rights leader)

Hopefully, after reading those inspiring quotes, you are entertaining new thoughts into the realm of the impossible. To further help you get there, I want to share seven practical methods God has established for you to enhance your imagination and increase your ability to believe.

Actively pursuing each of these can make all the difference in the world, so you can make all the difference in *our* world.

FILM

Watching movies that inspire you can jump-start your imagination and awaken your ability to believe in the impossible. By witnessing the lives of people who've accomplished notable achievements, you inevitably encourage yourself to do the same.

Whether it's a documentary or a drama based on a true story, film is an extraordinary medium for unleashing the greater potential that lies within you. I purposefully watch movies and documentaries that help fuel my own dreams and inspire me in some manner.

> *Life's like a movie, write your own ending. Keep believing, keep pretending.*
>
> ~ Jim Henson, American puppeteer and creator of the Muppets

BOOKS

Reading helps unlock your imagination perhaps like no other medium, by granting you direct access to the greatest hearts and minds in human history.

When you take the time to read about inspiring people who have accomplished tremendous undertakings, it helps you form a picture in your own heart and mind of what you might possibly be able to achieve.

> *Books are the carriers of civilization. Without books, history is silent, literature dumb, science crippled, thought and speculation at a standstill.*
>
> ~ Barbara W. Tuchman, American Pulitzer Prize-winning author

Reading transports you to any era of civilization so you can hear directly from the people of that culture. Throughout the ages, human beings come and go, but their words live on forever to inspire subsequent generations.

Nonfiction, inspirational, historical accounts, and memoirs are excellent genres to help broaden your scope of knowledge and expand your imagination. A good book could very well be the catalyst for your ascension into the world of the impossible.

MUSIC

Music is one of the most powerful forces God has given us to help us entertain limitless possibilities. Here's an amazing example. When Albert Einstein was asked about his theory of relativity, his response was, "It occurred to me by intuition, and music was the driving force behind that intuition. My discovery was the result of musical perception."

As a musician, I can attest to the inexplicable power of music. I use it regularly to stimulate my own creativity in areas outside of music.

In fact, there is rarely a time when I am writing my books that I am not listening to some kind of music that inspires my soul.

Music helps release a creative flow in people. American music educator Charles W. Landon stated it this way: "Where speech fails, then music begins. It is the natural medium for the expression too strong and deep to be expressed in words."

Film director and Star Wars creator George Lucas once said, "The sound and music are 50 percent of the entertainment in a movie."

There is simply no way to deny the incredibly powerful role that music plays on the human experience.

The profound inspiration I get from these musical passages always leads me to a place in my heart where I can once again be in awe of God's creation and begin to entertain limitless possibilities.

> *Music gives soul to the universe, wings to the mind, flight to the imagination, and life to everything.*
>
> ~ Plato, Greek philosopher and mathematician

OBSERVATION

Another great way to expand your imagination is to observe people who excel at what they do. By doing so, you are educating yourself and flooding your heart, soul, and mind with wondrous possibilities.

As you watch accomplished individuals engage in their life's passion, it expands your imagination and gives you a vision of what is possible.

My wife absolutely loves cooking, and Renee is very good at it. One of the ways she increases her knowledge of the culinary arts and her cooking imagination is by watching the Food Network daily.

After years of observing some of the world's top chefs share their culinary insights, Renee has developed quite a cooking repertoire. You should see the way she has created her own signature spin on many of the dishes she was first exposed to on the Food Network.

Making the effort to educate yourself in an area that interests you is what enables you

> *If I have seen further than others, it is by standing upon the shoulders of giants.*
>
> ~ Isaac Newton, English mathematician and scientist

to see new possibilities within yourself. After witnessing excellence, you'll suddenly find yourself thinking new thoughts and expanding your imagination.

CONVERSATION

The synergy that comes from talking with others will result in the manifestation of some of your best ideas and biggest breakthroughs.

God uses personal relationship and collaboration as the vehicles to further develop your imagination.

The key to getting the most out of your conversations with others is to discipline yourself to do more listening than talking. When I finally learned how to do that myself, I discovered many of the answers I was looking for were revealed in those conversations.

No one individual has a patent on creativity. God has gifted all of us with creative abilities, ideas, intuitive perceptions, and revolutionary thought processes.

When you commit yourself to conversing with intelligent people, you will always walk away with valuable insight and an enlightened perspective that will help you access your own imagination and unleash your own potential.

> *Never tell a young person that something cannot be done. God may have been waiting centuries for somebody ignorant enough of the impossible to do that thing.*
>
> ~ G.M. Trevelyan, British historian and author

PRAYER

Prayer is perhaps the most powerful resource God has given you to expand your imagination.

Billy Graham, one of the greatest Christian evangelists of all time, put it this way: "Prayer is simply a two-way conversation between you and God."

During that conversation, God can awaken things inside of you that you never even perceived were there.

Every time I am in a creative slump or burned out by some aspect of life, I pray and ask God to help me renew my mind, recharge my batteries, and grant me a fresh perspective. I can testify that as I remain diligent to seek Him for what I need, He always comes through.

The time I spend in prayer fuels my spirit for the times when I must fight the real and sometimes overwhelming battles of life. Only then am I armored up, strengthened and recalibrated for the days ahead.

> *More things are wrought by prayer than this world dreams of.*
>
> ~ Alfred Tennyson, English poet

THE BIBLE

When you read how God performed miraculous deeds through regular people, you will begin to see yourself through God's eyes.

This paradigm shift in how you view yourself will help you unshackle the chains that have kept you from taking flight with God. I can think of no other text in the world that would do more to strengthen your ability to believe than God's Holy Bible.

It is filled with incredibly rich examples of what it means to walk by faith. And

> *We account the scriptures of God to be the most sublime philosophy. I find more sure marks of authenticity in the Bible than in any profane history whatsoever.*
>
> ~ Isaac Newton, English mathematician and scientist

> *Imagination is more important than knowledge. Knowledge is limited. Imagination enriches the world.*
>
> ~ Albert Einstein

the Bible provides you with the tools and inspiration needed to reawaken your own childlike faith.

By engaging in these seven activities, you will expand your own imagination and ignite a flame in your heart to become a true believer. Doing so will allow you to reach higher ground and become who God intends you to be.

OVERCOMING DOUBT

It's only natural to assume that those closest to you would be the first to see your potential and demonstrate faith in your abilities. Unfortunately, this is often not the case.

In fact, it's not uncommon for your true talents to go unrecognized or acknowledged by your peers, teachers, friends, and even your own family members.

When people know you too well, this can cause them to hold a limited view of your capabilities. I call this the curse of familiarity.

When those closest to you fail to recognize your natural abilities or demonstrate faith in you, it can bring about unsettling discouragement. Understandably, it can have an adverse effect on the way you view yourself, often preventing you from developing the gifts God has given you.

> *Courage means being afraid to do something, but still doing it.*
>
> ~ Knute Rockne, American football player and coach

Many of our disappointments in life stem from the desire we have to share our unique gifts with people who show no interest in what we have to offer.

Due to negative comments made by those who cannot see our potential, we often lack the courage to pursue the thing we were created for. Despite the doubts of others, it's imperative that you pursue the vision God has given you. Your future impact on this world depends on it.

Before starring in *I Love Lucy*, Lucille Ball was told by her drama instructors to consider another profession because they didn't feel she had what it took to make it in acting. *I Love Lucy* became one of the most successful and longest-running shows in television history.

> *I'm happy that I have brought laughter because I have been shown by many the value of it in so many lives, in so many ways.*
>
> ~ Lucille Ball

By courageously choosing to move past the doubts of others, Lucy arguably has been responsible for more laughter throughout the world than can be calculated. She continues to have the same effect on generation upon generation posthumously via reruns in syndication.

The recipient of countless prestigious awards, Lucy was nominated for an Emmy Award thirteen times, and went home with it on four occasions. Her gift made room for her to bring the joy of laughter to a world that has such desperate need of this kind of medicine.

Lucy once said of herself, "I'm not funny. What I am is brave." Indeed she was. And if we could be a bit more brave ourselves, what might we be able to contribute to this world?

Through a combination of skepticism, cynicism, doubt, fear, unbelief, and low self-esteem, people frequently second-guess what they're good at when intuitively they know what they feel drawn to doing and being.

Listening to the doubters instead of God causes them to lose faith in themselves and their ability to believe God for a purposeful and prosperous future.

Surprisingly, the people who know you less intimately can often discern your natural abilities without hesitation. Their unfamiliarity with you makes it easier for them to see the obvious.

Some of you have had parents, family members, friends, or teachers who did recognize your God-given talent and encouraged you to pursue it at an early age. If this is you, consider yourself among the fortunate.

But this is certainly not the case for everybody. Even so, you mustn't lose heart. Remember, the only place Jesus didn't perform miracles was in his home town of Nazareth. The people there didn't believe in Jesus because He was a familiar face.

> *No pessimist ever discovered the secrets of the stars or sailed to an uncharted land, or opened a new heaven to the human spirit.*
>
> ~ Helen Keller, American author and political activist

The general consensus was loosely, "Hey, how great could Jesus be? I mean after all, we know this man. He's from right here in town, so He couldn't be all that. I mean come on, really, he's just a carpenter for goodness sake."

Now you see why I call it the curse of familiarity. Jesus affirmed that a prophet is without honor in his hometown.

The locals' intimate knowledge of Jesus made it difficult for them to see what was obvious to a mere stranger. So it should come as no surprise that those closest to your heart might not see your potential or believe in you, either. The important thing is not to take it personally or let it define you.

Jesus refused to let the doubt and skepticism of others prevent Him from continuing to pour out miracles on the rest of the people who did believe. There were many attempts by the enemy to defeat Jesus, but they all failed because He stayed in close communion with His Heavenly Father.

That relationship empowered Jesus to move past the temptation to give up. You too must stay close to your Heavenly Father if you want to overcome the temptation to give up.

Jesus did not let the naysayers' lack of perception change how He viewed Himself, or prevent Him from fulfilling His divine purpose as Messiah.

> *I am the way, the truth, and the life. No one can*
> *come to the Father except through me.*
> ~ Jesus, John 14:6

Jesus modeled the example we are to emulate. Neither should we let the doubt, skepticism, nor unbelief of others prevent us from soaring the way God intends.

It's encouraging to know that those who *did* believe in Jesus were rewarded with great riches for their faith. You too have great riches to share with others as you courageously make use of your unique gifts.

Eventually, people *will* surface who *do* see your potential and demonstrate faith in your abilities. They just might not be the people you'd expect. You must learn to accept that reality and refuse to hold resentment toward those who disappoint you.

Even when everyone you're surrounded by doubts you, including yourself, God does not. He continues to believe in you throughout all your trials and tribulations. Most importantly, He gives you the power to believe in yourself.

> *You may be the only*
> *person left who believes*
> *in you, but it's enough.*
> *It takes just one star*
> *to pierce a universe*
> *of darkness. Never*
> *give up.*
>
> ~ Richelle E. Goodrich,
> American author

Believing in herself is what Olympic gold medal gymnast Gabby Douglas had to learn the hard way. During a guest appearance I made on the *Huckabee* show in New York, I had the pleasure of meeting Gabby. She is a refreshingly sweet and humble young lady with a smile that just doesn't quit.

While she was busy taping her segment on the show, I had the opportunity to talk with her mother, Natalie Hawkins, a strong woman of faith. During that conversation, I learned a few things about Gabby that inspired me greatly.

In preparation for the 2012 Summer Olympics, 14-year-old Gabby had to move away from her family in Virginia Beach, Virginia, and relocate to West Des Moines, Iowa, to train with former Chinese gymnast Liang Chow. Liang is a renowned coach and former trainer of Olympic gold medalist Shawn Johnson.

During one particular visit with her family, Gabby told her mother she wanted to quit and move back home.

She was homesick and burned out from the grueling training schedule. For the first time in her life, Gabby was beginning to have doubts about whether she could be a winning Olympic gymnast.

Natalie refused to let her daughter give up. Natalie reminded Gabby of the great sacrifice the family made to get her to that point and how hard she had worked since age 3 to have the opportunity.

Natalie prompted Gabby to remember how many people she would be letting down if she gave up, not to mention her own country. Gabby came extremely close to quitting—only seven months before the Olympic games would take place.

But in taking the biggest leap of faith in her life, Gabby allowed God to teach her how to trust Him and believe in herself once again. Gabby stuck it out, and it was a good thing she did. Gabby's destiny completely changed. And as a result, she prospered beyond her wildest imagination.

Gabby went on to win gold medals in the individual all-around and team competitions. At 16, she made history by becoming the first African-American female gymnast to win the individual all-around event.

Gabby quickly became a household name and global media darling. Her achievements allowed Gabby to share her faith and powerful story of overcoming with millions of television viewers. She became a much-needed positive role model and inspiration to young girls around the world.

Gabby's story serves as a reminder of how close any of us can come to missing God's dream for our life if we give up believing in ourselves and God's ability to strengthen us through the tough times. For further reading on Gabby, check out *Grace, Gold, and Glory: My Leap of Faith* by Gabrielle Douglas with Michelle Burford.

> *I give all the glory to God. The glory goes up to Him and the blessings fall down on me.*
>
> ~ Gabby Douglas

THE DAY THE DREAM ARRIVES

One of the most exhilarating moments in life comes when you overcome your own self-doubt and accomplish something other people didn't believe you could.

To experience this priceless feeling of jubilation, you must choose to walk by faith and do all you can to continuously develop it.

I can't begin to describe the elation in my spirit the day my first copies of *The Big Gig* book arrived at my house. I purposely waited all day to open the box. I looked at it from time to time throughout the day, knowing good and well what was inside.

I wanted to savor every moment leading up to the big moment when I would open the box and my vision would come to life.

My wife made a special celebration dinner and cooked one of my all-time favorite meals—spicy garlic shrimp linguine. Right before dinner, my wife, daughter, and son gathered around the dining room table and watched me open my dream.

I stared at my book in absolute amazement. Staring back at me was a gorgeous 400-page book of inspiration. It looked so beyond my own capabilities. But I knew God had faithfully gifted me with the ability and graciously provided me with the life that made the book possible. Throughout *The Big Gig* journey, I continued to believe Him for a successful outcome.

After everyone in my family passed the book around the dinner table, I shared a heartfelt prayer of thanks to God. I then gave a short speech to my children about the virtue of patience and the reward for believing and walking in faith. That night we celebrated the blessing of God's faithfulness.

In 2012, a year after the release of *The Big Gig*, it was voted book of the year by readers of *Drum!* magazine, and received rave reviews in a number of notable publications around the world. I couldn't have been more thrilled; something I worked so hard on was inspiring people globally.

If I had been willing to give up believing against all odds that this dream would someday come to life, then the destiny of all the people I was called to inspire through the pages of my book would have been altered.

Please, never underestimate the importance of the things God has called *you* to do, no matter how insignificant they may look to you. Every encounter and assignment you have in your life, no matter how great or small, is significant to God.

Whatever you do, don't give up on the visions God has given you, and never allow defeat to be an option. If God chose you to carry a particular vision, it's because He believed you could fulfill it. Now, it's up to you to believe that for yourself, and then walk it out by faith.

> We all have our own life to pursue, our own kind of dream to be weaving, and we all have the power to make wishes come true, as long as we keep believing.
>
> ~ Louisa May Alcott, American author

BELIEVE: A QUICK SUMMARY

- Your faith in God is the greatest gift you can give Him.
- Believing is the key to receiving God's promises for your life.
- God always responds to your faith in some manner.
- You must reignite a childlike faith to believe God for the impossible.
- Faith is like a muscle; it can be developed and enlarged over time.
- Your faith will always be tested. Passing those tests qualifies you for blessings that couldn't come any other way.

Your Personal Prayer

Dear God,

I pray that You would strengthen my faith so I might believe You in spite of what my natural eyes see. I ask You to forgive me for the times I doubt You and let the circumstances of my life take precedence over Your promises. I will seek to magnify You, and not the problems and obstacles in my life.

I will acknowledge that there is no power greater in the universe than Yours, and it is through faith that I have access to Your tremendous life-changing power. From this day forward, like a child, I will choose to believe in You, Your principles, Your promises, and in Your kingdom. Amen.

7

BEND

Remain Pliable

*Many are the plans in the mind of a man, but it
is the purpose of the Lord that will stand.*

~ Proverbs 19:21 (ESV)

*I*t's a *Wonderful Life* is one of the most beloved movies of all time. Released in December 1946, the timeless Frank Capra film is a mainstay during the Christmas season on television networks around the world.

Actor Jimmy Stewart plays George Bailey, a responsible man from a small town who dreams of big adventure and traveling the world. His dreams are shattered, though, when his father dies—leaving a disappointed George to manage the family business, the Bailey Brothers Building and Loan.

At George's lowest point, he wishes he had never been born. Through an angel named Clarence, George is given the rare privilege of seeing how his town would have turned out had he never been born. Clarence shows George the profound difference he made in many people's lives, and George comes to understand that true success doesn't always look like what we think it does. George learns that he truly does have a wonderful life.

Have you ever had your dreams and plans fall apart, and wished you were never born? I certainly have. During the most difficult times of my life, I wondered why on earth I was here.

Even though I consider myself an upbeat and optimistic person by nature, there have been occasions when I didn't want to be here at all.

It was during one of those self-pity parties that I had an epiphany of sorts. I'd like to share it with you because it can help you put your circumstances in perspective.

The revelation God gave me was that *nothing I could do would ever stop me from existing.* Not even committing suicide would allow me to escape from existence because I am a created being with an eternal spirit.

When I finally accepted the fact that I am an eternal being and can't escape life's battles, a seismic shift shook my thinking.

Once I realized turning back was not an option—and there was nowhere to run and absolutely nowhere to hide—I began to boldly tackle the challenges I was facing and allowed God to mold me into the man He wanted me to become.

Life has a way of naturally setting up barricades that try to keep you from your destiny. But be of good cheer. If you are willing to listen, God will always show you a way through, under, or over them.

For every door the enemy tries to slam shut and lock, God has a special set of master keys that unlocks each of them. All you need to do to gain access to those keys is spend quality time in God's presence, be obedient, remain flexible, and be willing to act courageously.

You must understand that the road to your destiny will be one filled with many twists and turns. You can never know conclusively in advance how you'll get to your destination.

Despite your sincerity, earnest intentions, diligent planning, and hard work, there will be many unforeseen obstacles you'll have to face. It's tough. It's life.

You live in a spiritually hostile environment known as planet earth.

And as you pursue God's dream for your life, you can expect to be met with extreme opposition.

It's essential during times of opposition to remain pliable in God's hands as He shapes and forges your destiny. Choosing to keep the soil of your heart soft gives God permission to correct, discipline, and redirect you in any way that furthers His purpose for your life.

> *There is little difference in people, but that little difference makes a big difference. The little difference is attitude. The big difference is whether it is positive or negative.*
>
> ~ W. Clement Stone, American author and philanthropist

Choosing to be flexible will help you avert the frustration that causes many to give up on their dreams. Learning how to bend is life principle No. 7.

One of the keys to bending well is to maintain a positive attitude during life's difficulties. Your attitude in times of great trial will determine your ability to resist the temptation to give up.

GOD'S PROVISION

When God gives you a vision for your life, you can count on Him to supply you with the necessary provision to accomplish the mission. But you need to understand that it will require your active participation and willingness to bend.

As you learned earlier, I grew up in a single-parent home with a mother who had the overwhelming task of raising seven children alone. Making ends meet was always a real struggle for my family.

But none of the difficulties we faced prevented God from placing big dreams in my heart. It wasn't like He was waiting to see how things panned out before deciding to give me those big dreams. God gave me the dreams despite my personal challenges, and then faithfully provided a way for me to move past those circumstances.

His dreams for your life are not governed by any personal situation that you may find challenging or limiting at the moment. God sees beyond what you perceive as limitations and into the realm of the future where He has already provided a way for you to move past those barriers.

To help me move past the financial barriers that tried to limit me, God faithfully provided me with opportunities to work starting in early childhood. I did every odd job imaginable and was grateful for each and every opportunity.

I cut the heads off chickens and plucked them; cleaned up yards; washed cars and dishes; swept out barns; painted houses; and sold everything from seeds and greeting cards to eggs and magazine subscriptions, plus a whole lot more in between. I worked at a music store, a restaurant, and the county fair. I was even a groundskeeper at a community college. For as far back as I can remember, I have always worked extremely hard.

> *Opportunity is missed by most people because it is dressed in overalls and looks like work.*
> ~ Thomas Edison, American inventor and businessman

Sometimes, the jobs God provides for you are simply a means of financial provision on the way toward your dream. In addition to paychecks, God used those jobs to help develop my character and teach me valuable life lessons that couldn't come any other way. The training helped prepare me for better positions that awaited me in the future.

God proves his faithfulness by supplying you with opportunities. You prove your faithfulness to Him by taking advantage of the opportunities—performing them wholeheartedly for His glory.

This develops your work ethic and a sense of gratitude that proves whether you are worthy and ready for advancement.

With this in mind, you must remain flexible and open to how God may choose to provide for you, because He can accomplish this in many ways. It may be through your own hard labor that He provides. It may be a door of favor that He opens for you.

God may even put it on someone's heart to randomly sow time, money, or vital information into you, enabling you to move forward with your vision.

This is why you must never let your present-day circumstances dictate your future or have the last word with regard to fulfilling your destiny. Only God Himself has the last word, and His word is always the same: "Trust in me."

Remember, regardless of your background or personal situation, your individual needs come as no surprise to God. He is fully aware of your dilemma and has all the known and unknown resources in the universe at His fingertips to help you solve your problems and move you forward.

> *Stay committed to your decisions, but stay flexible in your approach.*
>
> ~ Tom Robbins, American author

In my own life, I have never known in advance how God is going to provide the means for my sustenance. Neither have I known the exact path He'd take me on that would lead to my eventual victories.

What I do know is that He has proven Himself to be faithful countless times and continues to astound me in the ways in which He chooses to provide what's needed for me to fulfill my mission.

BE RESILIENT

Without exception, the storms of life will rain down on all of us. When they show up in your life, you must imitate the palm tree and not the oak tree.

A palm tree is made of soft and pliable wood. It's supple and inherently sways during a hurricane.

The oak tree is made of dense wood that is not malleable. When the hurricane unleashes its massive force, it stresses the oak with incredible pressure. And due to its inflexible nature, the oak tree cracks and eventually splits.

There are really only two ways people react in a storm or when facing disappointment or rejection. They are either willing to bend or unwilling to bend.

Those who learn how to remain flexible—even when life stretches them to the point of great discomfort—have a greater likelihood of seeing their dreams come to pass.

In encouraging you to remain flexible, I'm sharing with you examples of high achievers whose dreams didn't come together as they envisioned.

> *Notice that the stiffest tree is the most easily cracked, while the bamboo and the willow survive by bending in the wind.*
>
> ~ Bruce Lee, American martial artist and actor

- Considered one of the most creative people in history, Walt Disney was fired from his newspaper job because the editor said he "lacked imagination and had no good ideas."

- Albert Einstein didn't speak until he was three years old and didn't read until he was seven. As a teen, Albert dropped out of boarding school. Because he lacked the equivalent of a high school diploma, Albert initially failed much of the entrance exam to the elite Swiss Federal Polytechnic School in Zurich, Switzerland.

- Before founding Microsoft, Bill Gates and cofounder Paul Allen started a company called Traf-O-Data, which produced a device that could read traffic tapes and process the data. Their first demo failed because the machine didn't work properly, but the experience prepared them to eventually run the global empire known as Microsoft.

- Film director/producer Steven Spielberg was denied admission three times to the University of Southern California School of Theater, Film and Television.

- Every cartoon submitted by Charles Schulz, creator of the Peanuts comic strip, to his high school yearbook staff was rejected.

- Fashion designer Vera Wang's first ambition was to be a figure skater. She even competed in the 1968 U.S. Figure Skating Championships. But when Vera failed to make the U.S. Olympic team, she decided to change careers. Now she is one of the most successful designers in the world and has even created competition costumes for Olympic figure skaters such as Michelle Kwan and Nancy Kerrigan.

> *Trial and error is at the heart of all creative processes. If we want to promote creativity and innovation, we have to honor and accept mistakes, false starts and dead ends.*
>
> ~ Sir Ken Robinson, English author and speaker

If those wildly successful people gave up just because things didn't happen the way they expected, or when they wanted, they would have never made the indelible mark they eventually did.

When facing grave disappointment, many people doubt the route on which God is taking them. Then, due to a lack of faith and resilience, they decide to jump ship. As a result, those kinds of people never see the fulfillment of their dreams. And how sad it that?

When life's difficulties come, be wise. Do not insist on your own way. God wants you to learn to flow with the changes He allows rather than fight them. Think of it this way: when you're struggling and refusing to give up, you're in great company!

We tend to have this false notion that highly accomplished individuals somehow didn't have to struggle or that they discovered some magical path that allowed them to bypass rejection. But apparently, just like you and me, they, too, faced many obstacles and great uncertainty.

When Elvis Presley first started out in music, the manager of the Grand Ole Opry fired him after just one performance. "You ain't goin' nowhere, son," Jimmy Denny told the King of Rock 'n' Roll. "You oughta go back to drivin' a truck."

How many people know Henry Ford's first business ventures left him broke five times before he successfully started the Ford Motor Company?

Dr. Seuss's first book was rejected by 27 publishers before finally getting published. By keeping his attitude right, Theodor Seuss Geisel was eventually able to bring incredible joy to millions of children around the world through his 46 witty, creative, and ingenious children's books. If Dr. Seuss gave up, we wouldn't have *How the Grinch Stole Christmas!*

Those world-changers are not isolated examples by any means. In fact, it seems to be the same story with everyone who has accomplished something noteworthy. Despite repeated failure, they remained flexible and resilient.

This revelation should inspire you to not give up in the face of adversity. Be bendable so your dreams can take flight.

Now, I'd like you to give careful consideration to the following questions pertaining to your past and future.

> *Adversity is the state in which a man most easily becomes acquainted with himself, being especially free of admirers then.*
>
> ~ John Wooden, American basketball player and coach

5 Questions about Your Past

1. How were you inflexible when pursing your dreams?

2. Are failures in your past preventing you from moving forward?

3. How have you handled rejection and disappointment in the past?

4. How have you dealt with criticism in the past?

5. Can you think of something that happened to you in the past that stopped you from pursuing your dream? What did you do about it?

5 Questions about Your Future

1. How do you plan to overcome adversity in the future?

2. What is the greatest challenge you need to overcome so you can continue pursuing your dreams?

3. What is your plan for dealing with criticism in the future?

4. How do you plan to develop more resilience in the future?

5. How can you improve the way you handle rejection and disappointment going forward?

The more you accurately reflect on how you have handled these issues in your past, and the more thought you give to how you plan to deal with them in the future, the better your chances are of developing a preemptive strategy for success.

TRUST GOD

On the way to fulfilling your purpose, you will have to endure many difficulties. It's called life. Please understand that every experience, both good and bad, is preparing you for your ultimate calling and destination.

God will mold you through the various hardships you endure. And it's precisely this intensified training that enables you to be a highly effective agent of change in this world. If you allow Him to, God will use your deficits, dysfunctions, and even your misfortunes as a means to bless and inspire many.

> *Life is not easy for any of us. But what of it? We must have perseverance and above all have confidence in ourselves. We must believe that we are gifted for something, and that this thing, at whatever cost, must be attained.*
>
> ~ Marie Currie, Polish physicist and chemist

At three years of age, Louis Braille suffered an eye injury in his father's leather shop in Coupvray, France. The accident eventually deprived him of his sight. In 1819, 10-year-old Louis attended the Paris Blind School, one of the first such schools in the world.

As a student, Louis developed a hunger for knowledge, and desperately wanted to learn how to read. For a blind person, though, there was really no good way.

He made it his mission to find a way. Through a willingness to improve upon an antiquated system that was in place, Louis eventually went on to invent "Braille," a worldwide system of embossed type that allows blind and visually impaired people to read and write.

Louis died in 1852 at age 43, but his life was extremely fruitful. By 1916, his system had been adopted throughout most of the world and since then has been converted into numerous languages.

In 1952, one hundred years after his death, Louis Braille was officially recognized in France as one of the nation's heroes. The president of France, Helen Keller, and many other dignitaries walked in honor behind his casket as his body was reinterred in Paris in the famous Pantheon.

Even without his sight, Louis possessed more vision than most. He displayed courage and refused to let his misfortune prevent him from reaching his potential and making a positive contribution to this world.

> *Just because a man lacks the use of his eyes doesn't mean he lacks vision.*
>
> ~ Stevie Wonder, American singer and songwriter

God graciously gave you gifts and talents to make a significant difference on this planet. Choosing to remain flexible allows God to lead you toward the destiny He has chosen for you—in the way He sees best, and in His perfect time.

Being stubborn, insubordinate, and impatient will prevent you from soaring the way God intended. But remaining soft, supple, and willing qualifies you for greater increase, favor, and reward.

If you remain submissive to the will of God, you will inevitably pass the tests He puts all of His children through. When you do, you will surely live to see His miraculous power demonstrated in your life.

The recipe for your success then is an equal mixture of rubber band and brick. The secret to succeeding lies in knowing when to bend and when to stand firm.

Accepting the challenges God sends your way allows Him to retool, reshape, and recalibrate every aspect of the dream He gave you. I know if you're like me, you probably prefer the times in your life when things are easy—the times of prosperity.

But the truth is you will only grow and rise to your full capabilities during times of pressure. Physical muscles only grow when intense pressure is applied to them. Spiritual muscles only grow when the pressures of life become extreme. That tension produces faith, the divine spark that governs all human actions, reactions, and interactions.

Refusing to quit, and continuing to trust God through the periods of your life that are filled with frustration, tension, and pressure is the key to receiving His promises. This, of course, requires perseverance.

> *You will never be the person you can be if pressure, tension and discipline are taken out of your life.*
>
> ~ James G. Bilkey, American author

Perseverance is the decision to continue pursuing God's vision for your life when the visible trail you are on somehow leads you into the harsh wilderness and leaves you for dead.

If you are truly following God's plan and purpose for your life, then you must also trust that part of the plan involves His perfect timing for the launch of the vision He has entrusted with you.

When it comes to battle, God is the greatest military strategist of all time. In His infinite wisdom, He has an exact timing that yields the greatest possible assault on the enemy.

When I ponder on what this might look like, I envision one of those battle scenes from the movie *Braveheart*. In the film, actor Mel Gibson plays lead character William Wallace, a thirteenth-century Scottish warrior who led the Scots in the First War of Scottish Independence.

Throughout the movie, William mobilizes his people against the tyranny of the British nobles and takes on King Edward I of England. In perhaps the most riveting scene of the film, William gallops on horseback in front of his brave warriors just before an epic battle is about to take place.

With an impassioned sense of conviction, he delivers a speech so enthralling and riveting that it will literally raise the hair on your arms. His powerful words fill the hearts of his loyal men with the courage necessary to face death square in the eye.

As the enemy approaches, William gives his soldiers their last-minute battle strategy. He instructs them to wait until he gives the signal before launching their surprise military tactic.

With the patience of a skilled general, William holds his forces back to the precise second that will allow them to have the greatest possible impact on their adversaries. It is the art of war in which precision and timing hold the keys to victory.

In this same way, God will sometimes hold you back intentionally until the time is perfect for the release of the vision He has for you. He doesn't do this to frustrate you. Rather, He does it so you'll have the greatest possible impact. And only He knows the exact timing that will produce the most favorable outcome.

In the end, you must choose to trust God like an innocent child trusts his parents. It's really simple if you look at it this way. Enlightened parents have wisdom their children do not yet possess, and they make decisions for the good of their children based on that higher level of understanding.

In a similar manner, your Heavenly Father has knowledge and understanding you do not possess. Since He is all knowing, He purposefully and strategically leads you the way He does for your own good.

> God often takes a course for accomplishing His purposes directly contrary to what our narrow views would prescribe. He brings a death upon our feelings, wishes and prospects when He is about to give us the desire of our hearts.
>
> ~ John Newton, English sailor and author of the hymn *Amazing Grace*

Be wise and rest in the knowledge that God is God, and He knows how to lead His people. That includes you!

It's only when you look behind that you can see the tapestry God has been weaving out of your life and fully appreciate the journeys He takes you on.

It's a lot like looking at one of those mosaics up close. You can't really see the image being portrayed unless you step back and look at it from the appropriate distance.

You have no choice but to live in the present. Still, you can choose to trust God on a daily basis to complete the mosaic in a way He knows is best for your future.

As time passes, you'll see how He worked out those trials, tribulations, and all of that tension for your benefit. Then you will gaze upon what God was painting on the canvas called your life and begin to realize that what He painted was good.

BEND: A QUICK SUMMARY

- Remaining pliable in God's hands is the key to seeing His promises come to fruition.
- Your willingness to bend keeps frustration from destroying your hopes and dreams.
- Your attitude in times of great struggle will determine whether you will fulfill your vision.
- God uses the trials and tribulations in your life to shape your character, which qualifies you for increase, favor, and promotion. This helps prepare you to serve in His kingdom.

Your Personal Prayer

Dear God,
I pray for Your perfect will in my life, and I give You permission to mold me into all You created me to be. I ask for an ample dose of courage to undergo the shaping process that You deem necessary so I might bear more fruit for Your kingdom.

I ask You to sustain my efforts through increased persistence, perseverance, and patience which will allow me to endure all that I must, in order to live out the dream You have for me. Amen.

8

Life Principle #8

BE

Embrace Your Individuality

To be yourself in a world that is constantly trying to make
you something else is the greatest accomplishment.
~ Ralph Waldo Emerson, American author and poet

In the world of music, there are indispensable people who are known as arrangers. These highly skilled musicians are given the task of writing the musical arrangement for a particular piece of music.

Once the entire score is fully conceived in the mind of the arranger, he or she begins to write out individual parts that will be assigned to every musician in the group.

When musicians play a piece of music for the first time, they have no idea what direction the music is headed or how it will end. They are discovering it in real time, much like you are discovering God's plan for your life in real time.

No musician can successfully jump ahead of the music, because it must be played in the proper sequence of time for it to make sense. If a musician looks at her music as a stand-alone part, she would be unable to comprehend how her specific part fits into the overall musical score.

Life is a symphony, and God plays the role of composer, arranger, and conductor. You are the musician whom He leads through the score.

If you would commit yourself to playing the part that's written specifically for you—instead of trying to improvise your own riffs over God's masterful arrangement—you would find the music to be a lot more pleasant.

Let me put it another way. If you would simply choose to embrace the uniqueness of who God made you to be—instead of trying to be something and someone you're not—you would find your life more fulfilling as well as fruitful.

Just as the lead violin player of an orchestra must trust in what the arranger has written for him, you too must trust in the original person God created you to be.

When you view only one aspect of who God made you to be, you fail to see your significance as a complete individual. Plus, you miss out on the amazing way all of your personal attributes can perform together in the symphony of your life.

God has faithfully given you a variety of personal attributes that constitute the whole of you. He also summons other people to be part of the ensemble of your life and then leads them to play their part in support of you.

A song tells a story and so does a life. God is trying to tell a beautiful and original story through the orchestration of your life. If you cooperate as one of His musicians, you'll discover that song and then learn to sing it with all of your heart, mind, and sou—to the glory of God and for the betterment of mankind.

The most powerful person in the world is the person who knows his or her song and resists the temptation to sing any other. This person will surely fulfill God's purpose for his or her life and have the greatest impact on his or her generation.

You weren't an accident. You weren't mass-produced. You aren't an assembly-line product. You were deliberately planned, specifically gifted and lovingly positioned on the earth by the Master Craftsman.

~ Max Lucado, American author and preacher

Remember, you cannot thrive, nor can you live a purposeful life in someone else's skin, because God had very specific reasons for making you the way He did. And He likes you just the way He made you.

Being yourself and embracing the uniqueness of who you are is life principle No. 8 and the key to living a life of meaning and impact.

RECEIVING GOD'S LOVE

No matter what you do or how hard you try, there will always be people in life who just won't like you. Unfortunately, our world is filled with many judgmental people who will choose to reject you long before they confirm there is actually anything objectionable or unlikeable about you.

This is your good, old-fashioned case of judging a book by its cover, and one of the oldest of all human injustices.

I used to try desperately to win those people over, but eventually, I learned to accept I had no power to convince anyone to like me—nor would I want to invoke such powers even if I could.

The fundamental problem with manipulating others into liking you is that it would be impossible for you to ever really feel good about knowing it was not of their own free will.

Effort spent trying to win these people over is a waste of your precious time—time you'll never get back. The bottom line is that you have no power to persuade people, and God wants you to have no part of it. He wants you to look to Him and receive His one-of-a-kind love.

Life on earth is an emotional battlefield with land mines all around us, ready to reap a whirlwind of destruction on the unsuspecting. The enemy's job is to stir dissension into the heart of man toward one another by perpetuating strife.

This plays out in a host of hellish ways, beginning with wicked comparisons of every kind.

Sadly, there are people who will despise you if you are attractive and others who will scorn you if you're unattractive. Whatever physical category you fall into is of no importance, because either will cause a certain segment of society to distance themselves from you, which is both unfair and unfortunate.

The jealous will detest you if you possess wealth of any kind, and the pretentious will look down on you if you fail to measure up to their standards.

There are countless unfair and unjustified reasons why people will choose not to give you a chance—all of which stem from horrible insecurities that prevent people from loving one another the way God commanded.

If we could fathom the depth of God's love for us as individuals, it would eradicate every form of insecurity we have ever known as human beings.

If we all knew beyond a shadow of a doubt that God loves us just the way we are, and that we don't have to earn His love, this mind-blowing truth would set us free to be who He created us to be.

That freedom would enable us to truly love ourselves, making it possible for us to love others from a pure heart. Then, just as the Grinch's heart did in the classic Christmas tale, suddenly our miniaturized, rotten hearts would enlarge.

All of mankind desperately needs a heart transplant. But the problem with human heart donors is we're all tainted—some more than others, perhaps, but without exception, we're all imperfect.

We need God to give us His heart. Only then will we be able to love and accept ourselves and one another the way God intends.

Unfortunately, very few people understand God's immense personal love for

> *Darkness cannot drive out darkness; only light can do that. Hate cannot drive out hate; only love can do that.*
>
> ~ Martin Luther King, Jr., American leader of civil rights movement

them. Because of this huge deficit in their heart, they act out by trying to trump and belittle others.

TAKING INVENTORY

Inasmuch as there are unjustified reasons people may shun you, it's critical for you to consider that there may be legitimate reasons too.

Start by looking in the mirror, and address any annoying traits, bad habits, or character flaws that may repel others. Some of your less-than-honorable behavior may have been passed on to you genetically through your family lineage.

What might not be a genetic predisposition may have been learned behavior you picked up from those who reared you. If you have problems that aren't genetic or learned, it most likely means you're doing something of your own free will.

Whatever the case, it would benefit you greatly to make adjustments and correct anything that may be preventing you from being received by others with open arms.

> *The greatest discovery of any generation is that a human can alter his life by altering his attitude.*
>
> ~ William James, American philosopher and psychologist

The wise, mature, and humble will always take responsibility for their conduct and make a sincere effort to improve in every way possible.

Although you have no control over who you come from genetically, or what learned behavior you acquired in your formative years, you do have control now over your heart, attitude, actions, and the behavior you choose to display to others.

ACCEPTING WHO YOU ARE

Despite your personal challenges and obvious imperfections, there are many unique characteristics about you that are divinely ordained because your Heavenly Father created you that way.

It is precisely those qualities you should not try to alter. God chose the generation and family into which you would be born. He designed the unique race you would come from and even set the stage for the culture and region of the world where you would live.

He also created you with the specific mind, body, and spirit that you possess. He gave you the ability to express yourself in your own special way, and prewired you with specific gifts and talents to make a quantifiable difference in this world. In His great love, He gives to each of us different gifts and talents.

To some He gave the gift of curiosity and inventiveness, for without such gifts the world of man would never advance, and life on earth would remain uneventful at best.

God graced Robert Goddard with these sensibilities, and they enabled him to push past the known barriers of science. A climb up a cherry tree at the age of 17 would forever change Robert's life direction. While in the tree to cut down dead branches, he became captivated by the sky, and his imagination began to run wild.

Robert began to envision a device that could ascend into space, and he contemplated how it might work. His mind was literally a million miles away. Robert's daydreaming would later impact all who occupy this planet of ours.

Born in 1852, Robert recognized the potential of rockets for atmospheric research, and anticipated many of the developments that were to make space travel possible.

He has been referred to as the man who ushered in the modern space age, and is credited with building the world's first liquid-fueled rocket, which he launched successfully on March 16, 1926.

But like all visionaries who are able to peer into a future that no one else can see, Robert was often ridiculed for his far-out theories of spaceflight. Nonetheless, he stayed true to his convictions and to the person God made him to be. In doing so, he was able to leave a monumental legacy.

> *Every vision is a joke until the first man accomplishes it; once realized, it becomes commonplace.*
>
> ~ Robert Goddard

Robert Goddard died in 1945, and many years after his death he was finally credited as the founding father of modern rocketry. His pivotal work as revealed in *A Method for Reaching Extreme Altitudes* is considered one of the preeminent texts of twentieth-century rocket science.

The secret to launching yourself like a rocket and orbiting around God's purposes for your life lies in just being you and embracing the part of your spiritual DNA that defines you.

This is no easy task, for sure, and few people seem to have learned how to do it. The inability to simply be who we're supposed to be keeps many of us from ever reaching our full potential.

That's why I can't overemphasize the importance of learning to accept and celebrate the person God made you to be. You are unique and full of inestimable potential!

To successfully accept who you are and become the best you possible, you will have to dig deep into your own heart and ask yourself some very important questions.

Here are seven of those questions:

1. What do you think is preventing you from fully accepting the person God made you to be?

2. How can being yourself help catapult you toward God's purpose for your life?

3. How can being confident with the person you are benefit the world around you?

4. Why do you think it's so important to be who God made you to be?

5. Where do you think you struggle the most in being you?

6. What would it take for you to be comfortable with who God made you to be?

7. What are your most unique attributes, which distinguish you from others, and how can you further develop them?

Remember, there is only one you on this planet. And in this world that is desperately trying to beat the "you" out of you, it takes an incredible amount of courage to be something that comes so naturally. That something is you.

Legendary jazz trumpeter and music icon Miles Davis once mused, "Sometimes you have to play a long time to be able to play like yourself."

> *There are three things extremely hard: steel, a diamond and to know one's self.*
>
> ~ Benjamin Franklin, a founding father of the United States of America

Even though he was expressing this sentiment in reference to a musician discovering his signature sound, it is a profound truth that applies to all.

It can take a long time for you to discover who you really are, and equally as long to get comfortable with the person you discover. When you finally ascertain what distinguishes you from others—and walk in the uniqueness of that truth the way God intended—your confidence will skyrocket, and your previous limitations will disintegrate.

> *Today you are you!*
> *That is truer than true!*
> *There is no one alive*
> *who is you-er than*
> *you!*
> ~ Dr. Seuss, American author and cartoonist

You should never allow people to change the person you are just to please them. We are all unique in our own right.

This should come as no great surprise since God has never made the same person twice. Have you ever heard of two people having the same fingerprints? Nope. At the end of your life, none of those people who tried to prevent you from shining the way God intended will be there to judge you.

You will have a solo audience with Him who sits alone on the throne. Knowing this, you should only concern yourself with God's opinion of you, rather than being swayed by the opinions of complete strangers.

Most of us give people way too much power over us. If you are ever going to be exactly who God made you to be, then you need to make a conscious decision to take that power away from those who try to exercise their will over you.

> *Your time is limited,*
> *so don't waste it living*
> *someone else's life…*
> *Don't let the noise of*
> *others' opinions drown*
> *out your own inner*
> *voice. And most*
> *important, have*
> *courage to follow your*
> *heart and intuition.*
> *They somehow already*
> *know what you truly*
> *want to become.*
> ~ Steve Jobs, American entrepreneur and co-founder of Apple Inc.

My father-in-law used to say to me, "You know what people are going to say about you, Z?"

"What?" I responded.

"Whatever they want to," he dryly replied.

Man, that is so true. People are going to say whatever they please, and there's absolutely nothing I can do about it.

When you can get to a place where you care less about what others think or say about you, it will be like drawing a "Get out of jail free" card from the game of Monopoly. It will free you to go about your business and pursue with complete confidence that which God has called you to do.

LIVING TO PLEASE GOD

Once, there was a man who learned to consume himself with absolutely nothing except pursuing the presence of God. Unlike most people, he did not concern himself with the opinions of others.

Rather, he lived only to please God. By doing so, he had the most profound impact on the people of his generation and every other subsequent generation.

Nicholas Herman, who later became known as Brother Lawrence, was born in France in 1611. It was while gazing at a barren tree in winter that he began to sense the extravagance of God's grace. He became so overwhelmed with a deep love and gratitude for God that he gave his heart to Christ.

He was 18 at the time. From that moment on, an intimate relationship began to blossom, which would continue to escalate throughout his life. As a result of this encounter with God's presence, six years later he served as a lay brother in the Carmelite monastery in Paris.

Brother Lawrence was an uneducated man, and because of that, he was unable to become a monk as he had hoped. Instead, he was assigned to work in the kitchen. Due to the heavy demand placed upon his schedule, Brother Lawrence was seldom released to attend the scheduled community prayer meetings and worship services.

Nonetheless, he decided not to let that stop him from pursuing deep intimacy with God. He turned the kitchen into his sanctuary. There in the busyness of his work, he began to develop a way of life he called Practicing the Presence Of God.

It wouldn't be long before others in the monastery began to take notice of his heartfelt devotion to God, and the ensuing radiance and peace that emanated from within. Brother Lawrence walked with such an aroma of love that his countenance was literally transformed.

He was so transfixed on communing with God that few could resist the opportunity to be in this man's presence. One by one, the monks in the monastery began to visit him in the kitchen, seeking words of encouragement and wise counsel. He seemed to have just the right word for the right occasion.

> *A good character is the best tombstone. Those who loved you and were helped by you will remember you when forget-me-nots have withered. Carve your name on hearts, not on marble.*
>
> ~ Charles Spurgeon, British pastor and author

In one of his most well-known statements, Brother Lawrence said, "The time of business does not differ with me from the time of prayer; and in the noise and clatter of my kitchen, while several persons are at the same time calling for different things, I possess God in as great a tranquility as if I were upon my knees at the blessed sacrament."

By dedicating himself to the Lord and remaining true to the person God intended him to be, Brother Lawrence was able to have a far greater impact than many of the more educated and revered clergy whose company he often kept.

When dignitaries of the highest order would come to visit the monastery, they would ask to see Brother Lawrence. Even though he didn't hold lofty degrees of higher education or an elite status in society, God made a way for this man to be a tremendous source of inspiration, because he was fully committed to Him and to the service of others.

> *The eyes of the Lord search the whole earth in order*
> *to strengthen those whose hearts are fully committed to him.*
> ~ 2 Chronicles 16:9 (NLT)

It was this simple man's wisdom and earnest passion for pursuing the presence of God that ignited a flame in the hearts of so many. After Brother Lawrence's death, Father Joseph de Beaufort compiled the wisdom that Brother Lawrence shared with the monks in conversations and letters.

It became the basis for the book *The Practice of the Presence of God*. It quickly grew in popularity and has become one of the most beloved books of the Christian faith. For more than 300 years, it has inspired generations with its powerful revelations.

> *God has infinite treasure to bestow... when he finds a soul penetrated with lively faith. He pours into it His grace.*
>
> ~ Brother Lawrence

When you can fully accept the person God made you to be and give that person wholeheartedly back to God as did Brother Lawrence, it will set you on a course toward the greatness for which you were created.

Then you'll be able to make the most of your life and the unique opportunities presented to you.

Remember, God has made only originals and you deprive the world of an incredibly unique and wondrous experience when you try to become someone other than the person you really are.

> *Make the most of yourself, for that is all there is of you.*
>
> ~ Ralph Waldo Emerson, American author and poet

Each of us has been assigned a noble mission. But it's like Cinderella's slipper in that the mission is custom made. I encourage you to be yourself because—in case you haven't noticed—everyone else is already taken.

DISCOVERING YOUR TRUE IDENTITY

When you begin to internalize who you are as a child of God, and better understand your identity in Christ, you will instantaneously carry yourself in a different manner.

You will walk around with a heavenly sense of confidence, which will be reflected in the way you do life. This sense of destiny will set you on an unbelievable path to glory.

I'd like to paint a word picture for you to illustrate a very important point. Let's pretend for a moment that we're the twin children of some powerful mega-billionaire. How about Bill Gates?

As young children, we set out on a great Indiana Jones-style adventure with our father to some remote land.

While on this journey, somehow I tragically got separated from you and our father. Despite all the search party rescue efforts, I was lost in a vast jungle and left to be raised by primitive tribes.

You, on the other hand, were raised with Bill as your father. You grew up understanding exactly who you were and where you came from. By the time you reached your teen years, you knew good and well how powerful your father was and what you stood to inherit one day.

This gave you an inner confidence and power to pursue whatever you felt led to do, with great expectation of future success.

I grew up an orphan, a pauper, a nomad with no understanding of my family lineage—barely surviving and in no way thriving. I grew up with no sense of direction or belonging.

But then one day by sheer accident, my whereabouts were finally discovered. In his great love for me, our father never gave up looking for me. And since he had tremendous resources available to him, he had search parties looking for me all those years.

I was finally brought home as a young adult. In the comfort of our father's palatial mansion, I began being groomed with the wisdom of our father.

He appointed his best counselors, teachers, and trusted advisors to prepare me to work alongside him. For the first time in my life, I began to see real potential for my future, and a hope I had never known.

The only difference between the two of us was that you always knew who you were and understood your true identity. I did not, and I couldn't envision the possibility of a more abundant and purposeful life.

We were both heirs to the same father, to the same earthly kingdom. And we had the same rights. Only you had a huge advantage because you knew our father and understood the fine print of your life. You read the contract—the living word—and were shown examples of what it was like to walk with great power. You were given vision and I was not.

And while this is only a fictitious story, I believe it clearly illustrates how two people with the same father and inheritance can have such vastly different viewpoints about their identity.

If you perceive this story through a spiritual lens, it demonstrates the difference between a person who understands his true identity as a child of God—heir to the kingdom and co-laborer with Christ—and someone who is utterly clueless as to where they come from, and what power and resources they have available to them at all times.

If you don't understand who you are and what you stand to gain by being adopted into the family of God through Christ, then you will wander the earth aimlessly with no vision, power, or hope for a better future.

To better understand your position in life and the rights and promises you have through your Heavenly Father, you simply must read the fine print of the contract. This is stated in God's Word—the Holy Bible—which still is the bestselling and most influential book of all time.

Our Heavenly Father, the Lord our God, owns all the cattle on a thousand hills. He owns everything in the land, sea, and sky. He owns everything that can be seen and everything that cannot be seen in the known universe.

He has more resources than anyone can imagine and they're available to Him at all times to give His children who call Him Lord and trust in His mighty name.

I implore you. Get to know your Heavenly Father because He loves you more than you can possibly imagine. Become acquainted with His ways, for they are not burdensome. Discover your true spiritual genealogy and heritage, and read the last will and testament to see what He has left you as one of His heirs.

You'll be glad you did. And when you do, you will inevitably fall in love with Him, for He is the essence of love and all that is good about life. What you uncover through this process will transform you into a person who walks with great love, power, and authority—one who can literally change the world!

For he chose us in him before the creation of the world to be holy and blameless in his sight. In love he predestined us to be adopted as sons through Jesus Christ, in accordance with his pleasure and will.
~ Ephesians 1:4-5

BE: A QUICK SUMMARY

- Your greatest strength lies in being yourself.
- Not everyone will like you in this life, and you must learn to accept it.
- The key to your effectiveness is to simply be who God made you to be.
- No one can be a better you than you.
- Embracing the uniqueness of you gives others license to do the same.
- Your true identity is that you are a child of the living God, adopted through Christ Jesus into the family of God, and created for a divine and noble purpose.

Your Personal Prayer

Dear God,

I pray that You would remove the blinders from me so I can see myself the way You see me. Help me embrace the unique gifts, qualities, and personality You gave me to impact this world. Show me how I can be all You created me to be so I may fulfill my purpose and reach my full potential.

I ask that You heal all of the hurts and pains of my past, which have been inflicted upon me by those who have rejected me in some way. Give me the courage and freedom to be me. Teach me how to walk in Your ways so I might live a life worthy of the call You have placed on me. Help me to love myself the way You love me, so I can love others the way You love them, and love You the way You love me. Amen.

9

Life Principle #9

IMPACT

Make a Difference

A life is not important except in the impact it has on other lives.

~ Jackie Robinson, first African-American
to play Major League Baseball

Traveling the world over as a rock 'n' roll drummer definitely has made for an exciting life. It truly has been more than I could have ever asked for or dared imagine.

Yet my biggest and best goal in life has been and still is to follow God so I can have as much impact as possible for His glory. The rest fades in comparison.

That means I've remained open to how God wants to use me during the different seasons of my life. It requires seeking God daily and asking what His will is for me. It involves holding onto cherished dreams and plans, but not too tightly. It also requires me to go when God indicates it's time to venture forth into the unknown for reasons I can't see.

In 2005, I was pursuing the presence of God, and God handed me a powerful vision, which knocked me off my feet. In the vision, three words appeared on a huge flag blowing in the wind high up on a flagpole. The words were "Build My People."

Those three words impacted my spirit in a profoundly purposeful way. I sensed He was beginning to shift the direction of my life toward the ultimate destiny He had prepared for me.

One special lesson I've learned through the years about God getting ready to move me into the next thing is *fasten my seatbelt because it's going to be a wild ride.*

Sure enough. I had a dream during the next year in which I felt God telling me to sell my house and trust Him. Willing to follow the voice of the Lord, I put my home on the market. The house sold within a few months. In July 2007, I took a huge leap of faith and moved my family to Nashville, Tennessee.

Understand that my wife, children, and I were Californians through and through. My wife Renee was born in Northern California near San Francisco and had lived in L.A. since she was a young girl. The sand and surf lifestyle of West Coast living is truly one of a kind, and we were all about it.

Our children grew up wearing flip-flops, shorts, and sunglasses almost year round. Visits to the beach and Disneyland were part of our regular routine. We took sunny blue skies and swaying majestic palm trees for granted.

Yet, we left California behind. We said farewell to our friends, family, and everything that was dear to us to walk into the unknown.

Nashville has a hip Third Coast vibe to it, and we were eager to check it out. But when we arrived in July, we were met with record hot temperatures and humidity so thick we could hardly breathe. We weren't in breezy L.A. any longer. Even so, I knew God had me by the hand, so I was confident about where He was leading us.

God did an amazing work within our first week of moving to Nashville. I was offered an adjunct teaching position at Belmont University as a percussion instructor. I wasn't even looking for this job.

It was just one of many signs God showed me along the way that confirmed He was orchestrating my steps. As I followed Him by faith, God kept showing me His favor.

The teaching opportunity brought me into close relationship with many young people who I was able to impact in a positive way. A growing desire to impact more young adults throughout the world began to burn deep inside me. For the next two years, I sought the Lord to get clarity on how specifically He wanted me to impact the Millennial Generation. Eventually, the vision of how to build God's people became crystal clear.

In 2009, I founded Zoro International Ministries. The goal of the nonprofit organization is to equip young adults with the tools needed to succeed and live out God's plan for their lives. I would still continue to perform, record, teach, speak, and write in a variety of settings. But now the focus of my life would transition from being a performer to becoming a world changer.

God is still using all of my gifts and talents, but now He is assembling them in a unique way for greater impact. It's happening in a way I could not have foreseen. And that makes it all the more exciting and adventurous.

Since moving to Nashville, God has opened many doors for me, which have led to a vast array of newer assignments, opportunities, alliances, and friendships. He birthed brand-new visions and set up divine appointments in Tennessee that simply wouldn't have come together anywhere else.

In fact, it was God who directed me to write this book so I could impact even more people with my life's experiences.

Undoubtedly, God will have similar plans for you to impact people for the sake of His glory. Those plans won't look the same as they do for me. Yet they will still be powerful, and you will still need to listen for His voice and follow His lead.

THE DIFFERENCE YOU CAN MAKE

The New Oxford American Dictionary defines impact as, "The effect or influence of one person, thing, or action on another."

In essence, impact is making a difference in the lives of others.

Nothing moves the human heart more than seeing good deeds being carried out by our fellow brothers and sisters. When we observe people having impact—engaging in noble efforts founded in love—it has a way of impacting all of us. That's why living a life of impact is life principle #9.

All genuine impact stems from three important Bible verses. In Matthew 22:36, Jesus was asked which of the commandments was the greatest. His reply, in verses 37-39, was, "Love the Lord your God with all your heart and with all your soul and with all your mind. This is the first and greatest commandment. And the second is like it: Love your neighbor as yourself."

God pre-wired you with the capacity to love. Since all good deeds flow out of a heart of love, it's your job to choose to operate in it. Following those two commands found in Matthew—loving God and loving others—is the key to living a life of impact.

Blake Mycoskie is the founder of TOMS Shoes. As part of his company vision to be socially responsible and make a positive difference, Blake developed an innovative business model known as One for One. For every pair of TOMS purchased, the company donates a new pair of TOMS shoes to a child in need.

> *Do all the good you can, by all the means you can, in all the ways you can, in all the places you can, at all the times you can, to all the people you can, as long as you ever can.*
>
> ~ John Wesley, British theologian and author

TOMS has provided 10 million pairs of new shoes to children around the world. The TOMS program now also involves eyewear—for each pair of eyewear that is purchased, TOMS helps restore sight to needy people. The company says more than 200,000 people have been recipients of eye care.

TOMS even has expanded with the TOMS Roasting Co.—for each bag of coffee that is purchased, TOMS will provide a week of clean water to a person in need somewhere in the world.

"I believe each of us has a mission in life, and that one cannot truly be living their most fulfilled life until they recognize this mission and dedicate their life to pursuing it," said Blake, who is passionate about inspiring young people to help make a better tomorrow by encouraging them to give today.

Another person doing good whom you might recognize is Bono, lead singer of U2. I met Bono in Hollywood many years ago on the set of a music video shoot I was performing in. When filming was completed, we chatted for a while. I liked him straight away and found him to be a humble man with a strong sense of moral conviction.

It didn't surprise me in the least to see Bono go on to become one of the world's most famous philanthropic entertainers. He became a leading advocate for a variety of social and political issues including the fight against poverty and world hunger. In fact, the National Journal named Bono "the most politically effective celebrity of all time."

Bono has received three nominations for the Nobel Peace Prize, and was knighted in 2007. He was also on Forbes' Generous Celebrity List for his work with Debt AIDS Trade Africa, which works against the spread of AIDS and for debt relief in that country.

> *When you align yourself with God's purpose as described in the scriptures, something special happens to your life.*
>
> ~ Bono

Even though he is a mega rock star who could see the world revolving around himself, Bono is a stellar example of someone using his high-visibility platform to invoke positive change and make a mark with high impact.

Mahatma Gandhi, anti-war activist and primary leader of India's independence movement, is often quoted as saying, "You must be the change you wish to see in the world." Blake and Bono are certainly putting those words into action, and I congratulate them both.

What kind of change do you wish to see in the world? What do you feel God is leading you to do to make a difference?

Before you put this book down and attempt to be that change and make that difference, be sure to take inventory of your own life by doing a little self-examination.

The brilliant Greek philosopher Socrates said, "The unexamined life is not worth living." I endorse that sage advice and consistently look for ways in my own life to create impact that aligns with my gifts, talents, platform, and passions.

Regularly, I ask myself these five questions, and I invite you to consider each one for yourself:

1. What kind of impact am I having on others?

2. Am I seizing every opportunity I'm given to make a positive impact on others?

3. Am I willing to make a difference by investing my heart into one person at a time?

4. What are some specific ways I can impact the lives of others?

5. What worthwhile causes resonate in my heart and stir my passions?

BIG AND LITTLE DREAMS ARE
BOTH VALUABLE

Please don't get the idea you need to be a wealthy or famous person to impact others. You don't have to leave your family or quit your job to work in the inner city, or jet off to Africa to be a missionary.

All you have to do is be willing to make a difference by using what you have, and demonstrating love in your own personal way. You have gifts and talents, experiences and perspectives that can be of benefit to others.

Love has many faces and often shows up in simple and practical ways. Some things are small and simple; you do them because it's the right thing to do. How tough would it be for you to walk an old person across the street, encourage a friend who just went through a bad breakup, sit with a kid at lunch who everyone else is ignoring, or be a listening ear to someone who's going through a difficult time?

There are an infinite number of ways to impact people. All you have to do is keep your heart, eyes, and ears open, because opportunities to have impact are presented to you daily.

The truth is, most of us are deeply impacted by people who show us love in practical ways at times in our lives when we need it most.

I was 17 and had only been playing drums for a little over a year when I heard one sentence that would forever change my destiny. It came from Danny Wilson, the bass player of The Jeff Lorber Fusion, one of my favorite jazz-fusion bands at the time.

Being a very tenacious young man, I somehow finagled my way into the venue where the band was doing a sound check for their concert that night. Right after sound check was finished I asked drummer Dennis Bradford if I could play his drums. I wanted to showcase my drumming talents for him and the rest of the band to get some feedback on my musicianship.

Amazingly, he granted my request. When I was done playing for the band, Danny the bass player enthusiastically said, "Man, that was amazing. I believe you're going to be a superstar drummer one day."

Bam! Those words sounded a bell in my heart. That simple little sentence lifted my spirit to a place it had never known, and those words remained etched in my heart.

American soldier and author Claude M. Bristol reflected, "It's the repetition of affirmations that leads to belief. And once that belief becomes a deep conviction, things begin to happen."

That is exactly what happened to me as I replayed that one powerful sentence Danny said to me in my head countless times. This was especially helpful in the early days of my musical pursuits when my dream of becoming a successful drummer looked rather impossible. In those times of doubt, it really helped infuse a steady stream of confidence in me.

Can you think of a time in your life when someone did something kind for you or encouraged you in some way? Do you remember how much that impacted you? How it lifted your spirit and gave you hope?

Irish playwright George Bernard Shaw said, "If there was nothing wrong in the world, there wouldn't be anything for us to do."

How true is that? The world is full of problems and always will be. The good news is that God gives you the privilege of doing something about it.

> *There is no such thing as a self-made man. We are made up of thousands of others. Everyone who has ever done a kind deed for us, or spoken one word of encouragement to us, has entered into the make-up of our character and our thoughts, as well as our success.*
>
> ~ George Matthew Adams, American newspaper columnist

He endows you with the potential to create solutions and make a difference. Right this very moment, you can be the answer to someone's problem. Will you answer the call?

THE WAYS YOU SERVE

To make a difference in this world and maximize the impact you can have, you must first accept that your time here is limited and commit yourself to making the most of yours. Then you must come to the realization you were created to serve.

One thing's for certain: you *will* serve. The question is whether you'll serve God or yourself. The course of your entire life will be determined by the way you answer that one simple yet profound question.

When I think of a person who serves with all of his heart, I think of my friend Dr. Wess Stafford. Wess is the former president and CEO of Compassion International.

Compassion is a highly regarded Christian-based sponsorship organization whose goal is to make a difference in the lives of children who live in abject poverty. Compassion employees, volunteers, and sponsors work with thousands of churches in more than 26 countries—serving more than 1 million children.

Wess grew up the son of missionaries to the Ivory Coast and spent his boyhood in a West African village where he witnessed the cruel and horrific ravages of poverty. He attended a missionary boarding school between the ages of 6 and 10. Sadly, it was there that Wess was abused emotionally, sexually, and spiritually.

Birthed from the darkest moments of Wess's life came his calling, purpose, and life's mission. Wess became a child advocate and has had incredible impact globally.

Upon learning about the noble work Compassion was doing throughout the world, I jumped in with both feet and became a spokesperson for the organization in 2006.

One of my most memorable visits was to Guatemala, where I was able to see firsthand how the lives of the poor were being helped by Compassion. I served meals to children, visited the homes of villagers, and played and prayed with families. I even performed a solo drum concert for the children and taught a few of them how to play some basic drumbeats. What I did was not complicated, but it brought joy and hope.

What compels you to take action? What noble and worthwhile cause tugs on your heartstrings? I encourage you to search your heart deeply for those answers and then get involved. Remember, the best investment you'll ever make is to invest in people.

During the early part of my boyhood, my mother lived with many physical and financial difficulties. She couldn't provide me with the opportunities and experiences she knew I desperately needed. In her great love, Mother signed me up with Big Brothers Big Sisters of America in Grants Pass, Oregon.

> *The true meaning of life is to plant trees, under whose shade you do not expect to sit.*
>
> ~ Nelson Henderson, Scottish rugby player

Between the ages of 10 and 14, I had the incredible blessing of being matched in the program with Bill and Beverly Large. They were a wonderful, loving, middle-class couple in their early 40s who didn't have children of their own. The Larges also took my younger brother and sister under their care.

Bill was a big, burly man who worked as a heavy equipment operator. He also had a gentle spirit, soft voice, and huge heart. Bill was kind, patient, understanding, and most of all fun!

Beverly was a fun-loving, nurturing, and intelligent woman with a beautiful laugh, great sense of humor, and amazingly adventurous spirit.

I had many magical first-time experiences with Bill and Beverly. They took me to my first football game and then out for my very first pizza. After discovering how much I wanted to go camping—remember my epic book-writing effort on camping?—Bill surprised me with a trip to the magnificent Oregon coast for my first camping trip. The Larges bought me all the necessary fishing gear and taught me how to catch my very first trout.

Not only did they graciously give me presents for my birthday and Christmas, they also attended my first school talent show where I played on a cardboard box with my hands since I had no drums or sticks.

After I left the Big Brothers Big Sisters program, Bill and Beverly went on to adopt five children. I remained friends with them for more than 40 years, until they passed away.

Bill, Beverly, and the Big Brothers Big Sisters program are among the primary reasons I feel so strongly about impacting the lives of others today. As a means of paying it forward, I became a national spokesperson for Big Brothers Big Sisters of America in 2008.

Since then, I've continued to share my positive experiences from their mentoring program at fundraising events around the country. It's truly an honor to give back to the organization that did so much for me in one of my greatest times of need.

Maybe you've had someone come alongside you and make an impact in your life. What can you do to show them honor and pay the goodness forward? Perhaps God is stirring your heart right now to consider coming alongside someone who could really use your love, kindness, and affirmation.

> *What you leave behind is not what is engraved in stone monuments, but what is woven into the lives of others*
>
> ~ Pericles, ancient Greek statesman

SO MANY WAYS TO MAKE A DIFFERENCE

I had the honor and rare privilege of spending a couple of days hanging out with Academy Award-winner Denzel Washington. After meeting him and finding out how much he loved to acknowledge and honor those who contributed to his life's success, I became an even bigger fan.

Many high achievers can trace the roots of their success back to inspiring teachers or mentors. Denzel does this in his book *A Hand to*

HELP OTHERS
SOAR!

"Zoro's ministry provides the insight and inspiration needed to live a life of impact."
–KEVIN SORBO
Actor, director, producer, and author
(*God's Not Dead*, *Hercules*)

Invest in People
Invest in ZIM

Partner with Zoro International Ministries (ZIM) today and help people discover, develop, and deploy their God-given gifts

HOW DO YOU BENEFIT?
By partnering with ZIM you will:

- Positively impact culture through biblically based books, programs, TV, radio, social media, and speaking engagements.

- Powerfully equip people with the tools needed to fulfill God's call on their lives. Doing so will empower an entire generation to rise up and serve God with courage, conviction, and confidence.

HELP MAKE A DIFFERENCE TODAY!

zoroministries.org/donate

Zoro International Ministries, Inc. is a certified 501(c)(3) organization. All donations are tax-deductible.

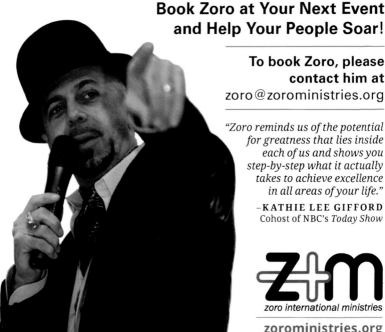

Guide Me: Legends and Leaders Celebrate the People Who Shaped Their Lives. Throughout his book, Denzel shares the stories of 73 leading personalities in sports, politics, business, and the arts. Each shares the story of how his or her life was impacted by someone who encouraged, inspired, and motivated them. Personally, Denzel gives praise to the Boys and Girls Club in Mount Vernon, New York, and club director Billy Thomas for giving him the confidence to succeed.

Today, Denzel is impacting the world not only through his acting but also as a national spokesperson for the Boys and Girls Club of America. He reminds people that they can make a difference by being a source of encouragement to someone.

Remember, a candle loses nothing by lighting another candle. Think about whom you might be a light to, and then be on the lookout for opportunities to help. I am confident you'll soon discover they're all around you.

They are many ways you can encourage people, but perhaps the most powerful way to do that is by the words you speak. There is no doubt that words shape us and have the potential to alter the course of our lives.

In light of that, you need to be very careful about what you let out of your mouth. Be mindful of the fact that once you say something you can never take it back. Use words to build people up, never to tear them down.

> *At the end of the day, it's not about what you have or even what you've accomplished. It's about what you've done with those accomplishments. It's about who you've lifted up, who you've made better. It's about what you've given back.*
>
> ~ Denzel Washington

Negative words can destroy confidence and taint self-image. I've spent all of my life trying to overcome the destructive words people said to me when I was young.

I bet you can remember verbatim the most hurtful things people have said to you and how deeply it affected you.

This is why, in the name of love, you need to train and discipline yourself to speak positive and affirming words to all you encounter. Life-giving words will be a tremendous source of encouragement and give you a practical way to positively impact absolutely anyone, anywhere.

A few positive words at the right time have the potential to change one's destiny. Listen to what encouraging words did for the famous Spanish artist Pablo Picasso: "My mother said to me, 'If you become a soldier, you'll become a general; if you become a monk, you'll end up as the Pope.' Instead, I became a painter and wound up Picasso."

> *Words are the most powerful drug used by mankind.*
>
> ~ Rudyard Kipling, English author and poet

Make no mistake, words carry with them great power. When you impact one person, you are potentially impacting many future generations. Talk about an amazing return on investment!

I refuse to waste a single opportunity to make an indelible mark on someone's life, no matter how small or insignificant it may seem. What about you? How are you using your time and what effect are you having on others?

> *I expect to pass through life but once. If therefore, there be any kindness I can show, or any good thing I can do to any fellow being, let me do it now, and not defer or neglect it, as I shall not pass this way again.*
>
> ~ William Penn, English minister and journalist

Everything you do and say is having some kind of impact now and throughout eternity. The key to all of this is to focus on doing the most good you can with the time you've been given. Simple.

DRIVEN BY ETERNITY

The only thing I'm interested in doing with my life is making a difference. Life is too short to pursue things that have no eternal value.

To do this, I must stay submitted to God in prayer so I can discern where He is leading me.

Far too many people pursue things they have no business going after—mindless and self-centered ambitions that are not directly tied to what God has called them to do. Consequently, they miss their true calling and the opportunity to make eternal contributions into the lives of others.

When God brought you to this earth, He established a personal account specifically tailored for you. It is one filled with a never-ending reservoir of love. That love will enable you to impact the lives of others to the very degree you wish.

There's no cap on the potential you have to make a difference because love can never be fully exhausted. And since God *is* love, He just keeps replenishing the account with Himself. Although you can never deplete what's in your account, you should live with the goal of being overdrawn by the time you reach the end of your life.

Living as if you're overdrawn in your love-for-others account will please God immensely and prepare you for heaven—the place where you'll be demonstrating your love for God and others throughout eternity.

Life here on earth is really nothing more than a dress rehearsal for the real concert you'll be performing in heaven. Start practicing now, and remember that you are part of a much bigger picture, part of a grand scheme, and just one of the many notes in a multipart symphony.

Without you, the music would be missing something. I liken it to one of the keys on a piano being broken. The song just won't sound the same without you.

So join the choir and sing your part with love, because the world is waiting for you, waiting for you to come alive and contribute something significant that God assigned only to you. Don't waste another minute being anything less than what you're capable of being.

Not everyone is called to be rich. Not everyone is called to be famous. Not everyone is called to win a Nobel Prize, run a Fortune 500 company, or win gold at the Olympics. But *everyone* is called!

> *We make a living by what we get, but we make a life by what we give.*
>
> ~ Winston Churchill, British Prime Minister of the United Kingdom

I challenge you today to rise up and make a difference, to look past your circumstances and deficiencies, and overcome your past. I challenge you to stop making excuses, living in fear, or waiting for others to do all of the accomplishing, impacting, and loving. I challenge you to be all God made you to be, to walk in love and take action now!

YOUR CALL TO TAKE FLIGHT

God wired you with the desire to soar in your spirit, and He placed within you a strong yearning to lift your heart toward heaven. The nine life principles listed in this book will enable you to leave the ground and get airborne.

This is the real flight you long to take and the true adventure you seek—knowing God intimately, sensing a bit of the divine, and fulfilling God's unique purpose for your life.

During an intense time of prayer, God showed me a vision that left an imprint on my soul. I was soaring through the air, far above the clouds, with Him alongside me.

It felt as if God was with me in the same way a skydiving instructor is harnessed to his student on a tandem dive. It was an exhilarating feeling of freedom that filled me with an unbelievable sense of confidence and well-being.

That picture has never left my mind, and it eventually became the inspiration for the title of this book and the framework for its contents.

I believe there was a divine purpose in that vision: for me to share it with you so you might picture yourself doing the same—soaring through the air alongside God to heights you've never known.

When times are tough and you feel like you'll never leave the ground, I want you to refuse to let go of that image of you soaring with God.

Picture it in your mind in your own personal way. This will help you persevere. Holding tight to God's promises for your future will allow you to experience the liftoff you so desperately desire.

To experience that liftoff, you must be willing to take risks. Every type of flight that man has undertaken involved risk. There is no way to push past your present-day barriers without venturing into the unknown. It will be risky and require faith.

Scottish author J.M. Barrie, best known as the creator of Peter Pan, stated it this way: "The reason birds can fly and we can't is simply because they have perfect faith, for to have faith is to have wings."

Increase your faith by trusting God; there is no other way. Refuse to give into doubt because with God all things are possible. He designed you with the capacity to take flight. It's your responsibility to develop your faith and get on the runway.

> *Formulate and stamp indelibly on your mind a mental picture of yourself succeeding. Hold this picture tenaciously. Never permit it to fade. Your mind will seek to develop the picture.*
>
> ~ Norman Vincent Peale, American minister and author

Like all good parents who want to see their children take off, God is rooting for you. The Creator of the world and your personal Heavenly Father wants to see you soar to the highest heights imaginable, and even to the unimaginable.

He wants to see you succeed, because He loves you! Take comfort in that fact, and don't forget you were made in His image. Since God is great, be confident that as His child you too have greatness inside you.

That greatness comes in the form of your creative potential—an unlimited potential that grants you the power to excel and take flight within the area of your unique gifts and talents.

Within you at this very moment is everything you need to succeed. And after reading this book, you are now equipped with a GPS that will help lead you to that success. There is nothing stopping you, so don't wait.

Go now. Go confidently. Go boldly and excitedly into the magnificent destiny that awaits you. Choose to make your mark on this world and make it a powerful, memorable one.

Before you close the pages of this book, I want to leave you with these final words of instruction: Think positive, believe with all your heart, work hard, be humble, pray fervently, act courageously, trust God, and always walk by faith.

If you do these things, you will soar high above the magnificent clouds with God, the one who loves you and wants to see you succeed!

Wishing you a passionate, powerful, and purposeful flight.

Zoro

IMPACT: A QUICK SUMMARY

- God created you to impact this world.
- God equipped you with the ability to make that impact so you can make a difference.
- God provides you with ample opportunities to be a source of encouragement to others through your love, kindness, deeds, and your words of affirmation.
- God created you for His pleasure and to soar with Him so you might accomplish the impossible.

Your Personal Prayer

Dear God,

I pray You would help me view all I do in light of eternity, and that You would awaken my spirit to all the opportunities I have to impact this world in a positive way so I can make a quantifiable difference with my life.

Show me how to be an encouragement to others, and please bring others along my path to encourage me. Perfect my faith and help me envision myself soaring through the air with You, so I might accomplish the impossible as You intend and bring glory to Your name.

And lastly, O God, grace me with the courage to be a true follower of Jesus Christ and compel me to live a life worthy of living. And after I have breathed my last breath on this earth, when my mission is completed, I ask that You would receive me into the gates of heaven so I may dwell with You there throughout eternity. Amen.

Your Personal Decree

In Proverbs 23:7, the Bible states, "As [a man] thinketh in his heart, so is he" (KJV). This means what you think of yourself is what you become. Earlier, I shared with you the powerful effect words have on shaping one's future.

What you become will ultimately be determined by what you think, what you do, what you say, what you read, what you watch, and what you believe. Since this is true, I want to give you this powerful decree as a life mantra.

A decree is an official order issued by a legal authority. God made you the legal authority over your own life when He gave you free will, so your decisions are the framework for your future.

Think of this decree as a spiritual manifesto for the vision you hold in your heart. I pray you will live out this decree by faith, and accomplish all God put you on this earth to do. Happy flying!

UNBEATABLE!

I am convinced that if I genuinely surrender my life to Jesus Christ, consistently submit to His authority, and do what He commands, I am UNBEATABLE.

No opposition can keep me from achieving God's dream for my life because all power in heaven and on earth has been given to Him who is able to do what He said.

This revelation gives me the power to believe that the impossible is possible, and to reach for God-size dreams that are much bigger than I alone can accomplish. It is my willingness to co-labor with Christ, and my desire to give my life away in the process—combined with my utter reliance on His strength and power—that will enable me to live out the dream He has placed in my heart and to soar with God.

Recap: 9 Life Principles

These principles help inform you of all you're capable of being, ignite a fire in your heart for God and his people, and help you discover His divine purpose for your life.

Keep in mind none of these nine principles are one-time acts; they are a way of life. Here is a quick glimpse at each of the principles:

Life Principle #1 – SURRENDER: Give Your Life to God
It's impossible to discover God's will for your life without actually knowing Him.

Life Principle #2 – DISCOVER: Identify Your Gifts and Talents
To reach your full potential, you must first uncover the unique attributes and special abilities God has given you.

Life Principle #3 – DREAM: Uncover Your Purpose
Once you know what your gifts and talents are, you can begin to dream about what you might accomplish with them.

Life Principle #4 – STRATEGIZE: Formulate a Plan
After you spend time entertaining dreams in your heart, you can then map out a plan for accomplishing them. Be sure you write in pencil so you can adjust those plans as the need arises.

Life Principle #5 – PURSUE: Take Initiative to Reach Your Dreams
Only after having a well-thought-out plan in place can you begin the actual hard work of pursuing your vision and moving toward it in an orderly fashion.

Life Principle #6 – BELIEVE: Live by Faith

To accomplish anything in this life, you must first believe you can. Everything comes down to developing the right thoughts and cultivating your faith.

Life Principle #7 – BEND: Remain Pliable

The road to your destiny will be filled with twists and turns, and inevitably your dream will be met with opposition. Remaining malleable will prevent you from quitting when the going gets tough.

Life Principle #8 – BE: Embrace Your Individuality

The only way you can possibly fulfill God's plan and purpose for your life is to be the person He created you to be—yourself.

Life Principle #9 – IMPACT: Make a Difference

The true purpose of your life is to make a positive difference in this world. You accomplish it with the resources, assets, background, gifts and talents, and personalized passions God gave you.

If you truly hope to succeed and reach your personal, vocational, and spiritual potential, then you will need to revisit, re-examine, and reapply these nine life principles throughout your life.

But don't wait for some magical moment before you decide to move forward with your dreams. Time waits for no one, and the clock is always ticking. Yesterday is gone, and tomorrow is a promise to no one. Today is all you have. Start now!

Many people die with music still in them. Why is this so?
Too often it is because they are always getting ready to live.
Before they know it, time runs out.
~ Oliver Wendell Holmes Sr., American physician and author

About the Author

Zoro

He is the consummate definition of the rare man who marches to the beat of a different drum.

Known as the Minister of Groove, Zoro is an internationally renowned rock star, motivational speaker, master storyteller, and author. Throughout his more than 30-year career, Zoro has consistently been voted the No. 1 R&B drummer and clinician in the world.

As one of the world's most respected and award-winning drummers, Zoro has toured and recorded with music legends such as Lenny Kravitz; Bobby Brown; Frankie Valli and The Four Seasons; New Edition; Jody Watley; Philip Bailey of Earth, Wind & Fire; Angie Stone; Vanessa Paradis; Sean Lennon; Lisa Marie Presley; Tommy Walker; Lincoln Brewster; Phil Keaggy; and Barlow Girl among others.

As author of the critically acclaimed and highly successful book *The Big Gig: Big-Picture Thinking for Success*, Zoro has equipped countless people around the world with the tools needed to succeed.

Richly gifted as an encourager and life coach on the subject of excellence, Zoro is a kinetic bundle of human energy and enthusiasm. The Minister of Groove is one of the most engagingly winsome people you will ever encounter. He captures audiences and readers around the world with his unmistakable trademark hip style, sense of humor, and contagious conviction.

His practical wisdom empowers and inspires everyone to reach the greatness that lies within. Zoro's genuine passion to serve led to him being honored at the nation's capital as part of the White House Fatherhood Champions of Change & Convening of Engaging Men and Boys. Zoro was among a select group recognized for promoting responsible fatherhood and mentoring of boys. Zoro is also a spokesperson for Compassion International and Big Brothers Big Sisters of America.

An ordained minister, Zoro also established Zoro International Ministries (ZIM). ZIM offers an indispensable program that helps young adults discover, develop, and deploy their God-given gifts in order to live a life of intention, impact, and adventure.

A powerful and purposeful communicator who is all heart and soul, Zoro connects with all generations simply because he's real, relevant, and relatable. The indelible mark he makes with his music, words, and life continues to have a profound impact on those who come across his path.

zoroministries.org

SUBSCRIBE AND SOAR!

To continue soaring with Zoro's latest words of wisdom
and inspiration, subscribe to his blog at
www.zorominstries.org/blog

and his YouTube channel at
www.youtube.com/user/zorothedrummer

Soar with Zoro: Practical Wisdom for Life

zorominstries.org

Invest in the Future

Partner with ZIM Today and Help People
DISCOVER, DEVELOP, AND DEPLOY
Their God-given Gifts

For we are God's handiwork, created in Christ Jesus to do
good works, which God prepared in advance for us to do.
~ Ephesians 2:10 (NIV)

Don't just stand in the bleachers, get in the game
and take action today!

facebook.com/zorominstries

twitter.com/zorominstries

instagram.com/zorominstries

pinterest.com/zorominstries

zoro international ministries
zorominstries.org